BUSINESS ON A PLATTER

Also by the author

Mrs LC's Table: Stories about Kayasth Food and Culture

ANOOTHI
VISHAL

BUSINESS ON A PLATTER

What Makes Restaurants Sizzle or Fizzle Out

First published in 2019 by Hachette India
(Registered name: Hachette Book Publishing India Pvt. Ltd)
An Hachette UK company
www.hachetteindia.com

SRD

ISBN 978-93-91028-19-0

Hachette Book Publishing India Pvt. Ltd
4th & 5th Floors, Corporate Centre,
Plot No. 94, Sector 44, Gurugram 122003, India

Typeset in Guardi LT Std 10.5/16.5
by R Ajith Kumar, New Delhi

Printed and bound in India by
Manipal Technologies Limited, Manipal

For Aaliya

CONTENTS

Introduction

THE POST-LIBERALIZATION BUSINESS

It was the turn of the millennium. I had just joined the *Indian Express* in Delhi, which had a sterling reputation for frank and fearless journalism in the country. As a cub reporter, I aspired to do big stories that would be 'meaningful' and make an impact on society. Tracking restaurants was certainly not on the agenda. Neither I nor any of my colleagues at that time nurtured any ambition to write on food.

My boss herself conceded that food was just 'half a beat'. Yet as the office newbie, it was this that I got saddled with. The team I had joined brought out the features page of *Newsline*, the *Indian Express*'s city supplement. The day I joined, there was a dire need for stories. I was sent to check out a new Awadhi restaurant – a modest establishment some home cook had opened in a middle-class residential neighbourhood.

It proved to be a happy chance. Lucknow, the centre of Awadhi cuisine, was in my blood. I had grown up in the city and belonged to a family that cooked and ate food quite similar to what the restaurant was serving. Making a judgement came easy. I must have done a competent enough job of reviewing shami kebab and pulao because one look at the article and my boss decided to thrust the task of writing a weekly restaurant review column on to me. Overnight, I became the paper's food critic and columnist – just out of college, with zero preparation for the task, save an upbringing that had inadvertently revolved around food in a family where almost everyone not only was an exceptional cook, but had strong opinions on 'good' and 'bad' cooking. (I wrote about this upbringing in my first book, *Mrs LC's Table: Stories about Kayasth Food and Culture*.)

I took on the task reluctantly – and only after being promised the more 'intellectual' art beat as well at some point in the future (there were more senior writers in that cluttered space). Soon, it became apparent that while I did enjoy writing about food and its creation and retail, the real problem was in finding enough restaurants to write about to sustain a weekly column.

New standalones opened infrequently – and most that did were unremarkable Indian-Chinese or Mughlai restaurants. I sometimes took autorickshaws to different neighbourhoods in the city just to scan signboards above shops for any openings. Every week was stressful, every other day involved a hunt for review-worthy spaces. I survived by the skin of my teeth, panning many, praising a few and wishing for meatier assignments.

Some weeks were easier. A splashy new restaurant opening at a five-star hotel would take care of our editorial needs. But considering there were just about half a dozen hotels in Delhi then, these occasions were few and far between in the three years I spent with the *Express*. There were many food festivals at hotels, most inordinately boring. Some contributed to my early gourmet education, offering glimpses of cultures from far and beyond – vine dolmas, pungent goat cheese, yakitori and teppanyaki (sushi was yet to go pop), classic American cocktails, and old-world wines that I learnt to swirl at the emerging phenomenon of pompous wine dinners. The column I valiantly tried to keep above such PR-led stuff. It was meant to be different from and more entertaining than what the two or three other writers in that space were writing.

Having set a goal to write about new or exceptional restaurants only – either refreshing or refreshingly horrendous – I was in a bit of a soup. India's foodscape was regrettably dominated by middling eateries (it still is, though evolving) and there was very little interesting, new stuff happening. Nine years after Liberalization and four years after the first McDonald's had opened in the country in 1996, India's restaurant culture circa 2000 was still sputtering to a start.

It wasn't as if we didn't have restaurants. The old Punjabi eateries that had come up in the 1940s and '50s and served tandoori and Punjabi-inspired food plus a mishmash of 'continental' were still around. The 1980s and '90s phenomenon of Indian-Chinese restaurants that served 'manchurian' and corn-floured, saucy creations were popular too. Most standalones that opened around that time often served these cuisines all together within family-style set-ups.

Some speciality restaurants such as Bukhara, La Piazza and Spice Route – at the high end of the price range and usually within hotels – did attract another set of diners, those who passed for Delhi's cognoscenti. But despite their popularity, dishes such as Bull's Eye (warm chocolate pastry hollowed out in the centre in which a scoop of ice cream is placed) or som tum were only special-occasion treats for even evolved diners.

The bar scene was being reinvented for younger consumers. Rick's had just opened in 2001 at the Taj Mahal Hotel, showing 'with it' Delhiites a way to lounge with cocktails and food instead of going clubbing at Djinns at the Hyatt, which was till then the most happening club around. Food was slowly becoming entertainment even in these nightlife places, but it would still be some time before it was finally recognized as a hero, and experience-led lounge bars with noteworthy food and drink (instead of just DJs and music) would start coming up.

A few other restaurants with food firmly at their heart were conversely trying to establish themselves as 'experiential' spaces, and these attracted the celebrity crowd. Places like Fujiya at Malcha Marg became known for the diplomatic crowd. Bistro at the Deer Park in Hauz Khas was frequented by the politically and fashionably connected, and Rohit Khattar's Chor Bizarre, which had opened just a few years earlier, was seen as quirky and arty. It saw the fashion, art and theatre crowds congregate and was quite the happening place in Delhi of the early 2000s.

The idea that restaurants were not merely about sustenance but were a larger experience was relatively new. After Liberalization, a new generation of Indians was gradually getting used to the idea of eating out for entertainment and to socialize, as opposed to filling a need or to marking a special occasion like a birthday or wedding anniversary.

The opening-up of the economy meant that there was rapid social change. Gen X and Y had already been in the midst of the first dot-com boom, people were travelling outside the country more frequently and students from middle-class families were aspiring to study abroad. In short, there was a thirst for more cosmopolitan, global experiences.

The late 1990s, when I was still in college, had begun to see young entrepreneurs with limited capital but some international exposure try to turn professional restaurateurs. These were not socialites or experienced businessmen. Their approach to restaurateuring was completely different. Some would begin to create restaurants for 'people like us' – for the young, informal, global new Indians. Restaurants that offered food chic and different from the dowdy 'family-style' standalones of the older generation – but which were not as pricey or stuck-up as those in five-stars tended to be. There was space in the eating-out market for the young, aspirational Indian and a few younger restaurateurs were beginning to recognize that.

While I still studied at Lady Shri Ram College (LSR), there had sprung up in our neighbourhood in East of Kailash a 'cafe' (though it was really a casual restaurant) with piri piri pasta, cheesy bakes, shakes, banoffee pie and other desserts that made us drool.

The Big Chill Cafe was set up by a young couple not much older than the college crowd, and became an immediate favourite with LSR girls, young IT professionals in the locality, their friends and friends of friends who kept recommending it to their peers. As word spread, the tiny cafe that was hard to find in a residential neighbourhood became quite popular, not just for its food but for its environment of casual chicness that was new to us in India – something its owners Aseem and Fawzia managed to create seemingly without effort. The category 'casual, upscale' was being birthed right before us.

It's been several years since I last spoke to them, but the couple's story remains fresh in my mind: Aseem Grover, an officer with the Indian Army, took premature retirement after he met and married Fawzia Ahmed, a Pakistani national based in London. They came back to Delhi and, with their combined savings of ₹8 lakh, set up Big Chill. Fawzia cooked, Aseem managed, and their small but modern business resonated with us '90s kids.

Big Chill was the first restaurant not just in Delhi but

possibly in India to hire young, English-speaking wait staff, many of them graduates from Delhi University, assured, confident and of the same socioeconomic strata as the young customers of the cafe. Till then, Delhiites had been used to the feudal bowing and scraping of old-fashioned, predominantly male 'waiters' in most family-style restaurants. Suddenly, Big Chill had introduced the very democratic idea of service staff at an equal social footing with the patrons. This was refreshing. With more people travelling today, attitudes to the service staff are changing in India with a much more casual service style adopted by many restaurants. In those days, this was highly unusual and Big Chill was a path-breaker. On busy evenings, when the service staff was hard-pressed, guests who had become friends with the owners would chip in to wait tables. It was all very American collegiate. There was none of the obsequiousness that people from an earlier India expected from restaurants. There were no white tablecloths or napkins; cutlery came in stands placed on the tables; there were plastic glasses, but the shakes in them were delicious – nothing like we'd had before.

For a brand that has endured for 20 years now and is so well loved, it is astonishing how Aseem and Fawzia are hardly ever written about. Theirs is the quintessential restaurant success story. Big Chill Cafe started out as exactly the sort of small, quaint, mom-and-pop business that so many of us dream of owning one day, only that day never arrives. In today's tough business environment, it would be very difficult to set up and sustain something like that. In this book, we will trace why anyone entering the big bad world of restaurants in India today should not come with the rose-tinted glasses that Aseem and Fawzia might have worn when they started their business. Two decades is a long time and the restaurant business is more grown-up, a big bad world for fledgling restaurateurs. Enter it with caution.

If Big Chill was slowly, and through word of mouth, growing in stature, 2000 saw one of India's brightest culinary stars till date bursting upon the Delhi food scene. Cappuccino, another small cafe near LSR, had been started in 1996 by a young Marwari girl with no restaurant experience but some serious cooking talent. The business did not succeed and she left for London. But by the time my batch had graduated from college and I had found work as *Indian Express*'s food critic, she was back in action.

A few weeks into my job, I was told of a new restaurant opening in Greater Kailash II, an area with a market known for its hardware shops. I entered Diva as its first reviewer to be fed new things like arancini and bocconcini by its very passionate chef, who bullied me into eating almost all of the menu, even as I took breaks to play chess with the then boyfriend in a part of the restaurant that had been done up with some board games. Even with my limited exposure to 'real' Italian food (Nirula's cheese-and-sausage pizzas was what counted as Italian then for most of us kids), I was blown away by Ritu Dalmia's cooking.

I came back to write a rave review – the first piece of writing about the restaurant. When that got published, my editor, Raj Kamal Jha, quipped, 'Boss, was it really that good or did you make it up?' I hadn't made it up. The proof is still in the pasta, almost two decades down the line.

Big Chill and Diva in Delhi, along with Indigo and Olive Bar and Kitchen in Mumbai (which came up in 1999 and 2001 respectively), ushered in a new type of restaurant in India. These can be defined as experiential restaurants, where a younger lot of diners went not just to satisfy a basic need for food as sustenance, but to meet an aspiration for a certain lifestyle these restaurants symbolized. The cosmopolitan Indian was just beginning to come into his/her own after the economy had opened up, and these experience-led restaurants would firmly become a big part of the metropolitan lifestyle.

Aviation, telecom, retail, travel and even hotels are sectors that have been studied in far greater detail as post-Liberalization businesses. Restaurants deserve the same attention too. How the industry has changed in the two decades or so since the mid-1990s is an equally visible symbol of change in the economic and social life of middle India and needs to be examined in greater detail.

This book will shed light on how this new business – of experience-led restaurants, cafes, bars, upscale diners – has evolved through these two decades. Because my career as a devoted observer of this space coincides neatly with the infancy-to-middle-age journey of standalone restaurants in

India, a business now in the midst of an unprecedented boom, I will attempt to offer insight into why some restaurants go on to become our favourites, why so many don't and what we can learn from the successes and failures of some of the biggest names in the Indian restaurant industry today.

Fledgling restaurateurs will find themselves surrounded by a host of advisers, some with no idea of the real nature of this tricky business, while others paint unrealistic pictures of the business.

Since I am neither a restaurateur nor a restaurant consultant, the idea is to offer a truthful, unbiased but subjective analysis in the good old journalistic tradition, cutting through the hype that envelops this business in India.

My analysis is based on my deep observation of this space for close to two decades, from a unique perspective of being both an insider and an outsider. My close acquaintance and friendships with many restaurateurs and chefs has given me a perspective of the business from the inside out. Many of these people in the industry, with whom I share mutual respect and camaraderie, have routinely spoken of their business in informal, unguarded ways, sounding me out on a variety of issues and seeking advice. Many of these conversations are built into this book and are the basis of my understanding of the business.

Then there is the journalistic training as a commentator that has always allowed me to spot new trends and patterns of behaviour almost as soon as they begin to happen, probe and question what different people in the business with diverse motivations tell me, and examine the business as an informed outsider – from the point of view of the consumers.

It is this unique understanding that I bring to you – a twin perspective that is advantageous when it comes to making sense of what really is happening in the world of Indian restaurants and in analysing what makes them ultimately work – or not.

from what different people in the business with diverse motivations tell me, and through my writings as an informed outsider—from the point of view of the consumers.

It is this unique understanding that I bring to you—a twin perspective, that is advantageous when it comes to making sense of what really is happening in the world of Indian restaurants and in articulating what makes them [illegible] work—or not.

PART 1

IN THE BEGINNING

Before we begin examining what makes upscale, experience-led restaurants in India succeed or fail, it is a good idea to get a sense of their history. While the boom in standalone mid-level casual restaurants is fairly recent and those in the business as well as consumers tend to think of India as a 'young' market, the chequered history of food retail in different restaurant formats is actually fairly old and has much to teach us.

What were some of India's earliest restaurants? A popular tale of Mughal romance gives us some answers. According to lore, when Jahangir met the future Noor Jehan (Mehr-un-Nissa) at a meena bazaar, a makeshift market in Mughal times to sell items or donate money for charity, she had her mouth stuffed with batashas, dainty meringue-like confections made from expensive refined sugar. Mehr-un-Nissa was a lady-in-waiting to the dowager empress Salima Sultan, Akbar's first wife, and had bought the batashas from a stall in the bazaar. These kinds of 'pop-up' bazaars, as we would call them today, were places where ladies from the Mughal harem set up stalls of crafts, clothing and food as entertainment for royalty. And these were typically held during popular festivals such as Nowruz, the Persian New Year, which, according to various historical accounts, were celebrated by the Mughals with great fanfare.

If these were royal bazaars meant only for the aristocracy, by the time Shah Jahan shifted his capital to Delhi, trade (including restaurant trade) was bustling in a very urbane way. In account after account on Mughal Delhi, including by travellers such as Niccolao Manucci from Venice and François Bernier from France, and later-day accounts by Indian poets and historians, we get a sense of Shahjahanabad as a highly evolved, cultured capital, where poets, artists, spiritualists and the finest of cooks congregated, right till the time of Bahadur Shah Zafar II.

Bernier in his *Travels in the Mogul Empire* describes a huge variety of foods, both uncooked and cooked, sold in the bazaars of Shahjahanabad. A culture of connoisseurship was developing and would continue till the very end of the Mughal empire. Stephen Blake notes in *Shahjahanabad: The Sovereign City in Mughal India 1639–1739* that coffee houses, or qahwakhanas, were places where poets would congregate, debate and read their works, earning praise from those gathered. This can be seen as an important milestone in food retail in India. This was perhaps the first time in metropolitan India that a cafe culture emerged – where a cup of coffee could be looked at as something promoting social and cultural interaction.

This emergence of the cafe culture is ironically seen as a modern phenomenon today, with co-working spaces within cafes and bars. The modern-day cafes as co-working or socializing spaces are as representative of a popular youth culture in Indian cities as the qahwakhanas were of old Delhi.

Shah Jahan's Delhi also had its khomchawallas (who sold snacky treats from cane baskets and moved from locality to locality), halwai shops (selling sweets, breakfast goodies and snacks), kebabchis (kebab makers) and naanbhais (bread makers), who cooked and sold the choicest of delicacies to the city folk. In the years to come, halwais such as Ghantewala would become iconic, even mentioned in various accounts of the Sepoy Mutiny of 1857 by citizens of Delhi, some of whom saw the sepoys as uncouth hordes who had descended on their urbane city and had become softened by its riches. As William Dalrymple writes in *The Last Mughal*, some of these accounts blame soldiers for being softened by the luxuries of Delhi and the sweets from Ghantewala, refusing to fight in the name of the emperor and in fact running away, leaving Delhi to be decimated by the retaliating English forces.

Meanwhile, khomchawallas, another set of peculiarly Shahjahanabad retailers, can be seen as mini 'moveable restaurants' akin to food trucks – they carried bamboo baskets from locality to locality to sell to their patrons dainty moong pakoris, chaat and daulat ki chaat made from milk froth every winter. This form of food retail continued to exist well after Partition, when families staying in old Delhi enclaves still patronized khomchawallas, the original chaat vendors of India.

Naanbhais, kebabchis and nihari shops were other retailers in Mughal India, not just in Delhi but also in other large cities that patronized food cultures under the Mughal influence, even as the power of the Mughal emperor himself was on the decline. In Lucknow, where Mughlai culinary sophistication was to reach its zenith, an old nihari shop, Rahim in Chowk, exhibited this ditty on a board, extolling the superiority of Lucknow's food over Delhi's: *'Janab Hazrat e Ghalib jab yahan aaye / pakar ke baith gaye woh Rahim ke paaye'* (loosely translated as: 'When Ghalib left Delhi to come to Lucknow, he sat down holding on to Rahim's dish of trotters').

Markets in cities such as Lahore, Hyderabad and Lucknow had entire streets devoted to food, full of small restaurants and famous cooks who specialized in a single dish. We see remnants of this kind of food retail even today. However, it is important to note that back then this was primarily the preserve of men, who ate and patronized street food.

Tunday Kababi, the popular kebab shop in Lucknow, is an example of this kind of retail. Though now gentrified and touristy, the shop was set up in the red-light area of old Lucknow by Haji Murad Ali (1877–1967), a migrant from

Bhopal. Ali was called *tunda* because he had only one arm. The original shop still exists in Chowk in the old city, though other outlets have opened. Early accounts of the shop by its patrons talk about how men would buy the kebabs made with beef, a cheaper meat than mutton that the more moneyed classes (both Muslims and Hindus who ate meat, like the Kayasths) ate, wrapped up in *dona*s (leaf cups), and walk up the dingy staircases to visit the prostitutes. A fond account of this slice of non-elite Lucknow life and Tunday Kababi has been written by Urdu poet Shabbir Hasan Khan (1898–1982), also known as Josh Malihabadi, in his autobiography *Yaadon Ki Baarat*.

Meanwhile, the gentility and women ate mostly at home. Till even the late 1980s and '90s, when I was growing up in Lucknow, *chatorapan* (the fondness of chatpata, frivolous restaurant food) was frowned upon, and women and girls from 'good' homes were not encouraged to go to restaurants. This is a social mindset that was completely demolished in post-Liberalization India.

Why restaurant food was not considered appropriate for genteel middle-class Indians might have had to do with the ritualistic way in which food has always been cooked in India. Food was treated as medicine, prepared carefully according to flavour combinations based in Ayurveda – the science of food and medicine, which recommended a balance of various *guna*s ascribed to each ingredient – and strict caste injunctions and rituals governed its preparations and eating in most upper-caste Hindu kitchens.

As I have written in my earlier book, *Mrs LC's Table*, brahmin women were employed to cook family meals in my community. They cooked only after having taken a bath and wearing clothes only meant for the kitchen. Such injunctions were followed across many upper-caste communities. The idea of 'purity' was important to high-caste Hindu families and eating 'outside', 'unclean' food was a no-no.

Some of these attitudes of Hindu society to food were clearly imbibed by the larger Indo-Islamic culture of Hindustan (areas of northern, eastern and western India dominated by the first six Mughal emperors). Even as early as Jahangir's time, Europeans who came seeking exclusive trading rights found themselves fondly welcomed, but none of the nobility – Hindu or Muslim – willing to eat with them![1]

Dining was a private affair for both Hindus and Muslims, who ate with their own kind mostly – and we can see traces of this sort of segregation even now. What this meant was that even in cities where food was elevated to an art form, the best fare was still what was cooked by highly paid chefs for an elite audience within homes.

If professional chefs run restaurants today, history has come a full circle. In medieval India, the moneyed nobility employed the highest-paid chefs and not the bazaar chefs who cooked the common man's chaat, kebabs and breads. Several accounts of Lucknow, including the early 20th-century *Guzishta Lucknow* by Abdul Halim Sharar, talk of highly paid rikabdars, or professional cooks, who specialized in unique dishes that left their diners amazed.

Shaikh Fida Ali was a rikabdar during the reign of Wajid Ali Shah, the last nawab of Awadh. He once placed a transparent lampshade on a table before a British dignitary. He placed a lit candle inside the lampshade, then blew it out, broke what appeared to be the glass of the shade and started eating it. 'It was later learnt that the entire lampshade was made out of sugar candy,' wrote Aslam Mahmud, an old Lucknauwallah and bureaucrat, in his superbly researched *Awadh Symphony*, which talks about life under the nawabs. Centuries before molecular gastronomy began to beguile us with its presentations, the rikabdars were already practising food as an art form.

Restaurant cooks, on the other hand, traditionally didn't know how to cook these nuanced dishes, and restaurant cooking has therefore always been distinct from home cooking in India. This fact is crucial to any understanding of the country's food- and restaurant-scape. For the first time, really, in the history of food retail in India, we are at a point where at least some restaurant food cooked by chefs is being considered more evolved and more desirable than home food. Experience-led dining that was confined to moneyed homes (as opposed to restaurants that were more functional and catered to mass needs) has only relatively recently shifted out of that private zone and into a public, social one.

After the British assumed power in India and Mughal might was lost, cooks who had till then laboured in the kitchens of aristocrats found themselves out of work. Some of them found work with new employers but discovered that these new sahibs and brown sahibs of the Raj did not understand the elite art. Chef Mujeeb-ur-Rehman, a well-known chef from Lucknow popular for his high-end wedding catering, tells me this delicious story behind the popular Lucknow idiom, '*Yeh moonh aur masoor ki dal*', used to be dismissive about someone.

According to him, a chef who found employment after having served a nawab for a long time asked his new employer what he would like to eat that day. The employer told him to make something simple like masoor dal. The chef in turn handed the employer a long list of ingredients to be bought for the preparation, looking at which the employer's face fell and he complained of the expense. The cook walked out, scoffing, '*Yeh moonh aur masoor ki dal*' (loosely translated as 'How can you, with this face, appreciate my masoor dal').

Used to a lavish, no-expense-spared way of cooking, the talented cooks must have been at a loose end. Some of them and their descendants set up small restaurants where they refashioned the elaborate and exquisite foods of their former masters as bites for common men. Qormas (hitherto cooked only within homes, nihari being the street dish), dal and pulaos were thus tweaked to become part of Mughlai menus at a few restaurants in cities such as Delhi, Calcutta, Lahore and Lucknow.

We find an example of this kind of shift in the story of Karim's, the iconic Mughlai restaurant in Delhi. According to his descendants' retelling of their restaurant's history, in 1913, Haji Karimuddin set up Karim Hotel in Gali Kababian near Jama Masjid, contending he was serving the 'food of royals to the common man'. Haji Karimuddin traced his ancestry to a family of Mughal cooks in Shahjahanabad that had to flee the capital after the last Mughal emperor, Bahadur Shah Zafar II, was exiled. The family relocated to Meerut. However, when India came under the British crown and the Delhi Durbar was being held in 1911, Karimuddin moved back to the city with the idea of opening a small restaurant to take advantage of the crowd that would be descending on the city for the durbar. Karim Hotel in the beginning served just aloo gosht, a home-style gravy of meat and potatoes, and dal to its patrons. The food was meant to be a substitute for home food.

In Calcutta, another cosmopolitan melting pot, dishes of Mughal origin were reinvented by small restaurants to cater to the needs of workers and daily-wage earners. Anadi Cabin on Esplanade is reputed to be almost a hundred years old. It has been around most certainly since before Partition, and remains unchanged till today, including in its use of the same iron tawa on which the cook shallow-fries Mughlai porotas (the Bengali term for paranthas), a beloved Calcutta street snack and Anadi's signature dish.

The tiny restaurant turns out 400 porotas from 20 kg of flour daily in a kitchen visible to all. The porotas could be covered in duck egg (which were considered vegetarian by traditional meat-eating Hindu Bengalis who did not prefer chicken) or chicken egg, filled with keema, folded and shallow-fried. These keema porotas are an innovation often credited to this restaurant. Mughlai paranthas almost certainly existed in Lucknowi and Awadhi homes before Wajid Ali's exile to Calcutta along with cooks who brought Nawabi dishes to the City of Joy. The simple egg-coated Mughlai parantha of Awadh, made with many layers or *parat*, underwent a metamorphosis to become the keema-filled substantial snack of Calcutta, which could be picked up easily and eaten on the go by daily-wage earners in the new city.

Many of these early restaurants thus came up as businesses that were seeking not to provide recreation but instead to cater to a need for cheap, filling meals as people moved from villages and smaller towns to the cities to work for their colonial masters.

However, colonialism in India brought with it more upscale restaurant and leisured experiences, catering to the elite.

The first passenger train in India started running between Bombay and Thane in April 1853, pulled by three steam engines Sahib, Sindh and Sultan on a 34 km broad-gauge line. As British India's rail network grew and the railways began to cover longer distances (Bombay to the capital in Calcutta was a much publicized route for first-class tourists), there was need for refreshments and restaurants en route.

Several British or Anglo-Indian travellers' accounts[2] speak of impeccable crockery, turbaned waiters and formal service, and food that was fairly similar all across the railways – thick soups, cutlets and bread and butter. It was, however, only Europeans or Anglo-Indian travellers who were entitled to travel in first-class carriages, and who could enjoy the catering in the dining cars. Conditions in the third class, in which the bulk of Indians travelled, were terrible. A 1929 *Times of India* report said that the Great Indian Peninsular Railways was trying out a separate dining car for Indians: 'It would probably not have allowed the third class passengers who made up the bulk of travellers, and who had to either eat food they had brought or buy at station halts on the way.'[3]

Since the catering was primarily for Europeans, European-inspired dishes started appearing on the menus in these restaurants along the rail network – things like chops, cutlets, omelettes, tea and custard. These dishes would eventually get absorbed as restaurant and club food in India, and we continue to eat some of this 'continental' food even today. The crockery and cutlery used were of the highest quality and the service by liveried waiters was impeccable, in keeping with the expectations of the sahibs of the Raj. Even after India became independent, upscale dining would imitate this pattern of deferential service.

While the dining cars were available only to first-class European travellers, from 1901, separate refreshment rooms for Indians started appearing at a few stations. This resulted in the emergence of other dishes that are now part of old-fashioned or nostalgic restaurant food centred around the Raj – for instance, the railway mutton curry (which clearly was never a single recipe) or the egg curry.

Till much after Independence, railway refreshment rooms were thought to be fairly high-standard restaurants, and railway catering would be relied upon for banqueting needs when dignitaries visited. My grandfather, who was in the catering division of the Northern Railways for some time in the 1970s, had amusing stories of catering to the Nehru–Gandhis – delicious anecdotes that we savoured as all restaurateuring tales must be.

But not all history is appetizing. The history of restaurants in India is fraught with caste and religious segregation – one reason that may have prevented a food retail boom earlier in the country's history. Once they started catering to Indians, railway refreshment rooms were segregated not just as those meant only for Europeans but also as those meant for Hindus versus Muslims. Even water from taps in the railway stations was marked Hindu or Muslim in British India.[4] There were 'pure' Hindu meals cooked by brahmins, and those offering Muslim food like qorma, kebab and pulao.

In the south, similarly, vegetarian brahmin hotels and 'military hotels' serving meat (with the suffix 'Hindu' added to signify that no beef or pork was served, though mutton was) came up as well as Udupi restaurants serving 'pure veg' food run by brahmins from the region, to cater to students and officers who worked in the Madras Presidency.

Restaurants like The New Woodland Hotel came up in the Madras Presidency, and can be credited as popularizing the Udupi-style food that continues to thrive today. Woodland, as it was popularly called, was set up in 1938 by K. Krishna Rao, a man from a poor family of priests from near Mangalore. Its customers then were primarily brahmins who worked for the government, or upper-caste religious travellers who were vegetarians. As we can see, for so much of their history, restaurants in India were not the inclusive businesses we see them as today.

Partition changed much of that. It rent India's social fabric in more ways than we can imagine. It unleashed bloody, religious violence, but with the old order being torn apart, space for the new was created. For the first time, as I argued in a 2017 article,[5] we got eateries that catered newly invented restaurant food to all manners of people – rich and poor, Hindu and Muslim. Butter chicken, dal makhani and naan became the first restaurant foods to escape the tag of religious identity.

Refugees from Punjab had arrived with less than nothing in Delhi. They brought with them a hardy spirit of survival and enterprise, but also one very important tool – the tandoor. A clay oven used to bake bread in villages, the tandoor made its foray into Delhi with refugees carrying memories of the sanjha chulha (the common village oven used to bake breads for all households) into this new harsh city where they had to fashion life afresh.

In 1947, an enterprising refugee from Peshawar, Kundan Lal Gujral, opened a restaurant called Moti Mahal in Delhi's Daryaganj area, in a building that had suffered badly during the rioting. Here, he set up a tandoor, in which the restaurant baked naan, a bread popular in old Peshawar eateries, and eventually chicken. The fowl was not a meat that Delhi was familiar with or fond of. 'Neither Hindus nor Muslims ate it, and initially there was some resistance to tandoori chicken,' says Anil Chandra, one of Moti Mahal's early patrons.

As food historian K.T. Achaya notes in his authoritative *Indian Food: A Historical Companion*, the chicken, as a scavenger, was thought to be 'unclean', and since the oldest of times, there has been resistance among brahmins and other upper-caste Hindus to eating its meat. Delhi and Uttar Pradesh's composite culture meant that these biases were ingrained in upper-class Muslim culinary cultures too.

Goat meat was prized and Mughlai dishes like shabdegh, silken qormas, gola and dil (heart) ke kebab, that required much dexterity, were made of goat meat within homes by specialist cooks for weddings and special functions. Specialist cooks like Hakim in old Delhi, whom old-timers told me about for my article for the *Wire*, and restaurants like Flora cooked these and catered to shaukeen, gastronomically indulgent

Dilliwallahs, both Muslims and meat-eating Hindus like the Kayasths. This courtly culture, however, waned after Partition as the Muslim elite moved away and refugees poured in.

The new tandoori chicken was India's original fast food. Simply done and fresh. Moti Mahal also takes the credit for inventing butter chicken: tandoori chicken pieces dunked in a tomato, yoghurt and butter laden sauce, and perhaps India's most famous restaurant creation.

The advent of this new kind of food served by Punjabi restaurateurs was to have a big impact on restaurant food everywhere in the country. In Delhi, restaurants such as Kwality, which had come up around the time of World War II and served ice cream and simple continental eats to American soldiers posted in Delhi, gradually incorporated this new Punjabi food into their menus. Other similar restaurants came up, also run by migrants, serving bold Punjabi flavours with tomato and cream, dishes that had been concocted within restaurants, and dishes such as pindi chana (a style of dry chickpeas popular in Rawalpindi) that came to Delhi and have been part of the city's most famous street dish since then – chole bhature.

After Independence, restaurants' clientele changed and Anglo-Indian and English dishes like cutlets, chops and scones were replaced or complemented by Indian snacks. As the years progressed and Punjabi enterprise started overtaking the traditional but conservative baniya businesses in different spheres, India's eating-out culture evolved. Unlike the conservative trading communities of the old order, who avoided eating out and were largely vegetarian, the Punjabi palate was willing to experiment. Bolder flavours within restaurants, meat dishes and alcohol all started becoming entertainment for the newly moneyed, who liked to spend on having a good time and be seen as spending too.

Camellia Panjabi, who was responsible for conceptualizing many restaurants at the Taj hotel chain in the 1970s, '80s and '90s, and for bringing street food to hotel restaurants much before this present trend of vada pavs on every menu, writes in her book, *50 Great Curries of India*, 'Attempts to introduce regional Indian dishes in menus always met with customer resistance, in the sense that customers continued to order the Punjabi dishes on the menu. In India, the majority who eat out as part of their lifestyle are Punjabis... Since they form the backbone of the clientele of almost every Indian restaurant in the country, restaurant owners are extremely wary of directing the menu away from Punjabi favourites.'

This may seem very different from the current context all around us, but till people like Camellia Panjabi at the Taj and Habib Rehman at ITC changed the game in the 1970s and '80s by introducing regional Indian food, Punjabi-influenced restaurant food dominated every Indian menu across the country, including at big hotel chains.

Panjabi finally did introduce local street food dishes and chaat from Mumbai at the iconic Taj Mahal Palace Hotel, and was a pioneer in the way she brought local street flavours to an upscale audience. But acceptability for this kind of local food came only after much resistance. She was the first to introduce street food in restaurants and forced chefs to cook regional dishes at Tanjore, which opened in 1973 at the Mumbai Taj. 'It was the first restaurant to serve pan-Indian food. Most restaurants were doing only Punjabi till then,' recalls the famous chef Hemant Oberoi, who began his career at that time.

Despite efforts such as these, from the 1950s to well into the 1990s, Indian restaurant food in hotels, in markets abroad such as London, as well as at iconic eateries such as Royal Café in Lucknow and Kwality in Calcutta, remained a mishmash of Punjabi and the older bastardized Mughlai. Much of it continues till today despite the rise of regional Indian food.

In the 1960s and '70s, however, as American pop culture gained influence among English-speaking, elite young Indians, dishes such as chicken a la Kiev (named after the Ukrainian capital but which got famous after Russian restaurants started becoming popular in the UK and the US) too made it to trendy restaurant menus. A new kind of 'continental' different from colonial and Anglo-Indian fare was born. But at the same time, another, far more popular cuisine was refashioning restaurant dining in India, spreading across the country from its city of birth, Calcutta – Indian-Chinese.

Records of Chinese settlers arriving in Calcutta, the seat of British power in India, exist all through the 19th century. As the British dismantled the remains of Mughal power and glory, new trade activities took root. Tea cultivation in Assam and Bengal was part of colonial enterprise and trade. Plantation workers from China, where the British already had a presence, were sometimes lured into coming to the gardens of Assam in the early half of the 19th century. A police census records 362 Chinese in Calcutta in 1837.[6] There were other migrants too, fleeing poverty or disasters. While some of the older migrants settled in Tiretta Bazaar – a busy market area named after Edward Tiretta, an Italian architect who designed it – later migrants settled on the eastern fringes of the city, in Tangra, a place where the tanneries had been set up outside the city since upper-caste Indians did not work with leather. The second wave of migration came just around the time of World War II and the Communist Revolution (on 1 October 1949, Mao Zedong proclaimed the establishment of the People's Republic of China). The Chinese community in Calcutta and parts of north-eastern India swelled.

Many of the Chinese immigrants earned their reputation not just as skilled leather craftsmen, supplying the British Raj with quality leather goods, but also as dentists, hairdressers and so on. Calcutta's Chinatown (the older one was in central Calcutta, the later one in Tangra) became the place to go to for early breakfasts, fish ball soup, steamed fish in soy sauce and the like.

Small restaurants run by the Chinese community sprouted up and would eventually unleash a dining revolution in India in just the span of a few decades. The food of the immigrants gradually began to combine with flavours appealing to the local Bengali palate. Eau Chew that opened in the 1920s in central Calcutta is today perhaps the oldest surviving family-owned Chinese restaurant in India – run by the fourth generation of the founding family, still fiercely protective about its recipes – and has been dishing out almost the same fare for close to a century, including the chimney soup it claims as its innovation.

Many of the small establishments once considered legends like Fat Mama's and Nanking have since shut. But the food that they ushered in lives.

As Calcutta-Chinese found wider appeal, other restaurants in the city and then in other cities around India started serving what we recognize today as Indian-Chinese. Deep-fried and sauce-laden flavours of dishes such as sweet and sour chicken, chopsuey, crispy spring rolls, chowmein and golden fried prawns have captured Indian hearts and palates ever since.

Chinese and Indian-Chinese food's growth was helped by its spread in the cosmopolitan Bombay of post-Partition years, a metropolis inhabited by the film and arty crowd that inspired fashions everywhere else. In the mid-1940s, Nanking was one of the few Chinese restaurants in Bombay. It may or may not have been an offshoot of the Calcutta Chinatown restaurant of the same name that had come up in the 1920s. There were about four or five other similar Chinese restaurants owned by members of the Chinese community in Bombay at that time. However, the owner of Nanking Bombay was crippled by gambling debts and ready to sell his business.

A Chinese immigrant named Yick Sen Ling who had settled in Bombay a few years earlier decided to buy it. With no previous experience in restaurants or cooking, Ling became a restaurateur. The rest as they say is history. Bombay's film set discovered Ling's food, as did moneyed Parsi and Sindhi families. He began to serve dishes like honey-glazed pork ribs and crabs (using local seafood from the western coast). Nanking's fame as a restaurant grew and along with it the popularity of the cuisine.

The 1962 war with China temporarily put a stop to this culinary fad. The Indian-Chinese community was looked upon with suspicion in the country and businesses suffered because of the negative sentiment. Many people migrated to places such as Canada – taking with them their culinary tropes.

However, as anti-China sentiments abated, there was no stopping the rise and rise of Chinese and Indian-Chinese. In the mid-1980s, Nelson Wang (born in a Chinese family in Kolkata) set up China Garden, where he would invent the chicken Manchurian, according to his own claim – a dish which is synonymous with the garlicky, chilli, cornflour soy-ridden flavours that Indian-Chinese is famous for. This would prove to be the new restaurant cuisine's iconic dish, luring many more customers who wanted something spicy, and even got a vegetarian version done like a kofta. In 1978, Delhi got its first Chinese restaurant inside a hotel by way of

House of Ming, which served Schezwan food, fierier than the Cantonese or Cantonese-influenced Indian-Chinese popular in Mumbai and Kolkata till then. All these strains would come together, and get further Punjabified in the succeeding years. At some point, the food would even get South-Indianized with a tadka of curry leaves. Noodles, Manchurian, spring rolls and sweet corn soup tweaked to regional palates would go pan-Indian.

There are a few big lessons we can learn from this history of restaurants from the Mughal era to right before modern India's economic liberalization. One is about inventiveness. Many restaurateurs tend to label Indian consumers as gastronomically unadventurous. This seems true if you see the kind of food that sells the most in the country: Indian, followed by Indian-Chinese, followed by Indianized pasta and pizza. Most markets in India have few restaurants serving international food, and diners generally are seen to stick to flavours they are comfortable with.

However, if we look closely at the history of restaurant food in India, it's clear that inventiveness has always worked. We have a legacy of dishes created specifically for restaurants – whether by way of the pepper-laced nihari cooked in the bazaars of Shahjahanabad, ostensibly to ward off the cold from the Yamuna waters, or the butter chicken that entered the national consciousness after Partition, or curry-leaf Chinese. What follows is also that the Indian audience has always recognized foods within restaurants as separate from dishes that are eaten at home. This is an important historical point to consider for any restaurateur.

Today, when regional Indian food is finding so much representation within restaurants, and chefs and home cooks are attempting to bring tastes of home into commercial formats, they inevitably come up against this deeply ingrained classification of food.

International restaurant trends are increasingly focused on local gastronomy, local ingredients and techniques of cooking in different parts of the world. The prime example of this would be a restaurant like Noma in Copenhagen, which opened in 2003 and brought Nordic gastronomy to the centre stage globally. Instead of the southern European ingredients and cooking that passed for European food in Scandinavia in the pre-Noma years, the restaurant and its highly influential chef René Redzepi shifted the attention to Denmark and local traditions of foraging and preserving foods through fermentation in the cold, harsh winters, and to indigenous ingredients (for example, using ants instead of lemons, which are not native to the region).

The influence of celebrated global chefs and restaurants looking at their own unique culinary heritages have shifted the attention even within India to our diverse regional foods and cooking traditions. However, when chefs attempt to plate up seasonal greens, homely and humble bottle gourd, pointed gourd, colocasia, pumpkin and so on that people in different regions of the country eat at home on a daily basis, there is a resistance from a mass audience to accept these within restaurants. Because of the way restaurant food has come up in the country, historically, a majority of consumers are reluctant to spend money on dishes and ingredients that they eat at home, however trendy these may get on Instagram thanks to popular chefs and restaurants championing the cult of the 'local'.

Opening a restaurant serving a specific regional Indian cuisine therefore is challenging – if a restaurateur is attempting to set it up in the same region (more on that later). The middle class in India, responsible for the boom in consumption, still cooks at home and is used to high-quality home food. Consumers look for what they do not regularly eat at home, the untried, the aspirational and the exotic within restaurants. Which is why if you go to a city like Ludhiana, a manufacturing hub in Punjab that is home to a community of very affluent business people, you will find that plush restaurants these days are all serving up novelty. I had martinis and sushi at RED, a high-quality Asian restaurant at the Radisson hotel there owned by the MBD group, whose home ground the city is.

Baba's butter chicken, from the eponymous small restaurant, which is the best-known dish in the city, and which may have inspired Pankaj Mishra's entertaining book *Butter Chicken in Ludhiana* on small-town consumption and aspiration in the 1980s, still does roaring business but it is not a homely dish. New restaurants are going beyond such well-known hearty flavours, with burger restaurants and cafes serving 'Western' food becoming more common. Then there are restaurants where the novelty comes not from food but from the experience – I spotted one housed inside the replica of an aeroplane.

In the metros, chains like SodaBottleOpenerWala or Social, which have plated up regional flavours in a pop way, or even a takeaway such as Goila Butter Chicken in Mumbai have all had success selling foods from another region to the audience of a particular city. Restaurateur A.D. Singh opened SodaBottleOpenerWala, inspired by the Irani cafes of Bombay, in Gurugram first because, as he had told me then, 'there is an immense nostalgia in Delhi for street food from Bombay which people recognize and may have eaten but is not easily available. Even those who have never been to Bombay and never eaten its street food or food of the Irani cafes still find it recognizable and aspirational'.

This has been key to the brand's growth. It has expanded to Mumbai too, but the resonance it has in other cities is far more.

There are full-fledged Bihari, Malayali, Assamese, Bohri restaurants in our midst today, in markets where there is either nostalgia or aspiration for these cuisines, not easily accessible to people in those markets and not cooked in their homes. But restaurants with specific regional or micro-regional cuisines must tread carefully; the novelty of these underexposed cuisines is what drives consumers to them in the first place, yet the food must be comforting and not wholly alien to the market, or people do not return. If you examine the menus of most successful regional Indian restaurants, you'll find how they balance the familiar with the exotic.

Diners may be attracted by Instagram posts, but because most Indian diners are still not evolved enough (I cover audience tastes in a later chapter), they quickly want to come back to the formulaic – with a twist. Jackfruit tacos are a good example – no different from rotis or thepla with some sabzi, but restaurantized.

This brings us to the second key point that becomes clear to us when we go over the history of food retail in India: India is a very old food culture, including when it comes to eating out, but most Indians are still new to restaurants as a leisure activity.

Restaurant-going in the way we think of it today was limited in medieval times to small sections of the population, and also food from the bazaars was always inferior to the luxurious courtly cuisines within the homes of the aristocracy. Spending on premium restaurants is a new phenomenon for Indians. Connoisseurship of the kind of luxury dining that existed before Partition primarily within homes was destroyed during the social and political upheavals of the past.

We have almost started from scratch in the post-Liberalization years when it comes to paying for food as highly evolved entertainment or art. The audience for quality restaurants thus seems immature in India when compared to many global food capitals. Within restaurants, millennials seem to seek more casual yet interesting bites, exotic yet familiar, but also seem to not care as much about quality as about price, willing to move away to the next new, shinier, cheaper restaurant with average food. To have patrons who want more from food than mediocrity, comfort or titillation at cheap prices – who want to be challenged intellectually by it, or who appreciate it as an art form and are willing to pay a price for that – will take some time. This is a theme that I will come back to later in the book. For, now, let us examine why some restaurants fail and why others succeed.

OF FAILURES AND SUCCESSES

One in every two people wants to be a restaurateur, design and restaurant mogul Terence Conran is famously credited with having said, while he still helmed a thriving restaurant empire in the UK, in 2005. Much has changed since then, but not the aspiration.

In 2018, Prescott & Conran, the business Conran set up with colleague Peter Prescott, has had to exit the restaurant business altogether.[1] It closed as many as six casual dining restaurants across London in the space of just a few months, resulting in many job losses. It is not the only restaurant company to have done so.

Even though global economies have been in a decade-long expansion since the global financial crisis of 2008, the restaurant business everywhere now seems to be struggling across segments. Popular casual dining chains such as Jamie's

Italian in the UK have collapsed (in May 2019, the restaurant chain announced that it is shutting 22 of its 25 restaurants, eating up 1,000 jobs, as widely reported in the British press). Carluccio, another chain of mid-level Italian restaurants, was forced to close a third of its restaurants in 2018. The BBC reported that 'in the year to 25 September 2016, even though revenues rose 2.7%, spiralling costs meant Carluccio's pre-tax profits fell by 81% to just £982,000'.[2]

It is now commonly accepted that the mid-market chain segment of restaurants, at least in the UK and parts of the US, two bellwether markets for restaurant trends, is distressed. There are also questions about how well the luxury segment is doing in many markets, with outposts of fine-dining restaurants such as Joel Robuchon Restaurant and Andre in destinations such as Singapore shutting down.[3]

Then, there are bars in India that we see routinely spring up but that shut a year or two down the line, once novelty wears off and customers gravitate to the next new thing in many markets. Sometimes, such restaurants try to inject fresh 'buzz' by changing name and look and feel, at other times, they sublet their space to another brand so that rent can be covered, while many simply shut after struggling for a year or more and even defaulting on rent. A property owner in Khan Market, for instance, told me how a restaurateur in that market had not paid rent for three years, even as the space for the restaurant saw two brands under different names come and go in that time. There are no studies around this phenomenon and it is not adequately covered in the food media in India, but close observers of the restaurant space are aware of this problem, as is the restaurant fraternity.

Finally, there are the small, single-outlet restaurants – their fate too is by no means certain, and many of these even in emerging markets are under pressure as rising costs, a tough regulatory environment and increased competition make the business tough.

In general, across segments and markets, profits in the business are slimming as many restaurateurs struggle to keep companies adrift in choppy waters. Rising costs – rents, wages and food – are also coupled with what many restaurateurs describe as erratic and changing demand of millennial consumers, making the restaurant business riskier than it was always deemed to be.

These factors have been afflicting many major markets (including India). In the UK, where 1,123 restaurant companies shut in 2018 (according to data released by the British Insolvency Service),[4] mostly high-street, upscale, casual dining restaurants, a report in the *Times* blamed millennials who frequent short-lived pop-ups instead of regular restaurants for this state of affairs. 'Fickle diners blamed as record number of restaurants go bust,' reads the headline, and the report goes on to talk about how 'diners seeking to impress friends by photographing themselves eating at trendy pop-ups have contributed to the collapse of more restaurant businesses in the first nine months of this year than the whole of 2017'.[5]

In India, most restaurateurs I talk to complain of grappling with the same phenomenon of fickle millennial customers: who patronize a newly opened restaurant deemed trendy on social media or within their social sets for the first few months and then quickly shift their loyalties to the next new 'buzzing' place that opens. This phenomenon can usually be observed in how customers seem to shift to new restaurant hubs such as the Aerocity in Delhi or BKC in Mumbai – instead of going to earlier popular hubs, where business seems to dip, as per anecdotal accounts. However, can this be attributed to fickle millennials or to oversupply of restaurants tapping into essentially the same pool of diners? That is food for thought.

The bulk of the restaurant clientele in India is definitely from the age group loosely described as millennials, but which is in fact quite a diverse audience, with many different subcultures. (A widely accepted definition for 'millennials' globally is those born between 1981 and 1996. This audience could be anyone from a 23-year-old to a 38-year-old, though some characteristics such as ease with technology, openness to new experiences and, in India, keenness to socialize at restaurants are common.) While there are broader similarities in patterns of behaviour and consumption, in different markets, millennials are different people and it is thus unfair to suggest that all are fickle restaurant customers.

Restaurant consumers today have more choice available to them, but there seems to be a problem of oversupply of restaurants in markets like the UK, coupled with wage stagnation for consumers, forcing people to spend less on restaurants. Unlike the *Times*, the *Guardian* in a November 2018 article on the same theme blamed 'high rents and business rates [and] a weaker pound' for the unprecedented number of restaurants failing (the failure rate in 2018 was up by a third over 2017, according to the Insolvency Service data).

The *Guardian* report was in particular damning about 'speculative private equity funds' fuelling failure. 'Thousands of restaurants have opened in recent years. Many, including some of the high-profile failures, have been fuelled by speculative private equity funds. These investors travel the country looking for "concepts" to "roll out". The logic is obvious. Restaurants cost a lot to outfit and open. A large cash injection allows for rapid expansion, while scale offers savings on cost. Inevitably some will fail,' it reasoned.[6]

In India, private equity has been fuelling much of the restaurant boom too – outlets of chains have been mushrooming in the metros and in places like Hyderabad, Goa and Pune. If done competently, this money can create wealth and growth – as we can see from the example of Barbecue Nation, India's most successful restaurant company in the casual dining space at the moment.

Barbecue Nation has grown from a single outlet in 2006 to 50 in 2016 and to over 100 in 2018 (according to a case study in the Food Services Report 2019 by the National Restaurant Association of India, or NRAI), making use of the investment made by CX Partners, a private equity fund that pumped in ₹80–90 crore in 2017. If it manages an IPO, as it has been planning (at the time of writing), it will be a validation of its business model, wherein a family-run business has successfully scaled using PE money and partnership.

However, not all restaurants funded by PE investments are healthy and profitable or able to deliver fair returns on investments. After all, the profit from a restaurant must be higher than if the investment had simply been parked in bank deposits, where fixed-deposit interest rates are 6–7.5 per cent per annum (as of August 2019), or mutual funds, where equity funds can deliver annualized returns of 10–12 per cent. A surprising number of restaurants in India today are not even able to deliver these kinds of returns despite all their glamour, something that many consumers do not realize.

We will look at the role of private equity in the restaurant space in India later in the book, but one common perception insiders in the restaurant business have is that to grow valuations and typically exit in three to five years, many funds allegedly put pressure on restaurant companies to go on adding outlets. And that some companies do this without paying adequate attention to their bottom line and store profitability, which is a key marker of financial health. This is obviously problematic. A brand may eventually collapse as it tries to cope with operational bandwidth, consistency and all the complexities human interface in a sensitive business such as restaurants involves, and yes, competition from similar players in an oversupplied market.

The funds, on their part, say that problems arise when the founder-restaurateurs themselves are confused about their models or unable to deliver what was promised at the time of funding.

Going by my observations, in many markets in the metros, there does seem to be oversupply and a lack of differentiation between restaurants based on quality instead of just price. As per the NRAI's India Food Services Report 2019, Indian consumers eat out just 6.6 times on an average in a month, much less than other Asian cultures in places such as Singapore (30 times a month), Bangkok (45) and Shanghai (60).[7] The NRAI report also mentions that households in its sample spent ₹2,500 on non-home-cooked food per month. Overall, this means that the average spend per customer per restaurant visit is quite low.

Indian customers are aspirational and want to frequent restaurants more frequently than ever before, but the amount of money they are able or willing to spend on every restaurant visit is low. So the more expensive restaurants such as those categorized 'premium casual' (average spend of ₹700–1,250) or 'pub, bar, cafe, lounge' (average spend ₹900–1,500) in the NRAI report will obviously have a challenge as they seek to sprout multiple outlets.

It is interesting to note that according to the NRAI report, affordable casual dining restaurant chains (average per person spend ₹350–700), the biggest category, surpassing even quick-service restaurants (QSR), in the organized restaurant business, grew at a compound annual growth rate (CAGR) of 18 per cent from 2015–16 to 2018–19, while premium casual dining restaurant chains grew 29 per cent CAGR in the same period. In the standalone space, affordable casual diners grew 12 per cent CAGR, while premium casual diners grew a whopping 34 per cent.

While there seems to be an audience for every kind of restaurant in India today, whether niche or mass, restaurateurs need to be able to gauge whether their restaurant models – specialized concepts, chefs as brands, enhanced food, drink and service experiences that would obviously entail a higher cost – are truly scalable or not.

The worrying slowdown being signalled in FMCG, auto, banking and other sectors of the Indian economy of late also does not seem to have impacted restaurants – as yet. Parle, the biscuit giant, may have flagged declining consumption for even its ₹5 per packet commodity, but restaurant consumption by urban millennials is still growing.

Restaurateurs are still optimistic, which is backed by macroeconomics to some extent at least. India is expected to become the world's youngest country with a mean age of 29, there is increased urbanization, and while 95 per cent of households earned less than ₹5 lakh in 2004–05, the figure shrank to 83 per cent in 2017–18. In contrast, households earning more than ₹10 lakh annually has risen from 2 per cent to 10 per cent in the same period, according to the NRAI report.

The fact that India is on its way to becoming the world's youngest country is a demographic advantage for the restaurant business, where younger consumers are becoming culturally more cosmopolitan and finding restaurants to fulfil social needs, unlike older generations for whom homes were the centres of their lifestyles.

Research firm Nielsen released a report in December 2017 ('What's Cooking with Indian Diners'), according to which, 'Young Indians, who comprise the middle-income millennial generation, newly entering the workforce, spend three times as much on restaurant visits than on any form of entertainment, including cinema, theatre, and other recreational activities.'

According to the report, the average annual spend for urban Indians on eating out was ₹6,500. In contrast, in the UK, the per person annual spend on eating out was £1,000 in 2017, according to a report on British consumer behaviour released by consultancy firm Kantar Worldpanel last year.[8]

Though Indian consumers have much catching up to do vis-à-vis global peers in terms of consumption at restaurants, what is interesting is how restaurant spends by millennials are higher than by the preceding Gen X. The Nielsen report mentions middle-income Gen X consumers spend just ₹4,461 annually on restaurants, while millennial middle-income consumers spend considerably much higher – ₹7,914 annually.

To cater to evolving, younger consumers, it is inevitable that the future will see many more experience-led restaurants and that India's restaurant culture will evolve in interesting and exciting ways. Clearly, there is opportunity for new restaurateurs.

This kind of big picture has led many players with no experience of the business to enter this space. In fact, it is impossible now to visit the neighbourhood chemist's or grocer's without overhearing talk of someone or other trying to set up a restaurant, cafe or waffle parlour!

For the aspiring restaurateur, it is important to pause and note that the picture is not as rosy as it may seem. While more and more restaurants are coming up on the premise of a lucrative business, and the number of experience-led standalones has gone up exponentially since my early reviewing days, restaurateuring in India itself has become riskier than ever.

This is primarily because of the high cost of rentals, long gestation periods for restaurants (most projects in India witness multiple delays in getting licences, clearances, etc.) that most newbie restaurateurs do not foresee, a lack of financing options (and high costs for domestic financing), unclear policies such as multiple clearances and high taxes, heavy import duties, different excise policies for different states and multiplicity and duplication of licensing at central and state levels to name just a few.

Then there are food and labour costs, which have been steadily climbing in India over the past decade. Despite these high costs, stiff competition and rampant undercutting constrain restaurants in most markets from hiking prices.

Sales are often driven by deals, all-you-can-eat offers, and unviable discounts pushed by food apps and reservation platforms, which in August 2019 resulted in a standoff between restaurants and online aggregators, when many restaurants in Delhi, Bengaluru and Mumbai chose to collectively log off aggregator sites, demanding an end to deep discounting.

The discount culture propagated by these aggregators, as well as by restaurants themselves, means that Indian consumers are spoilt for choice, though not necessarily quality-wise (since they learn to differentiate between restaurants on price alone), but restaurants bear the brunt, with very small or negligible profit margins. For instance, most Sunday brunches overloaded with champagne and caviar and goodies galore do not make profit for restaurants, occasionally making a loss even, according to industry insiders.

The less-cluttered Tier-II and Tier-III cities may, in fact, make for more viable markets for many types of restaurants, with more rational rents, and customers willing and able to pay to meet their aspirations. Within the larger restaurant markets like Delhi, Mumbai and Bengaluru, considerably higher costs and competition today mean that a mom-and-pop restaurant like what Big Chill used to be in the early 2000s, constrained by budget and set up by amateurs, has a considerably lower chance of survival.

A figure used liberally by many established restaurateurs to warn impetuous fools against rushing into this space is that, globally, the success rate of restaurants is just 10 per cent.

Which means, nine in 10 restaurants 'fail' in the first year. This is regarded as conventional wisdom, but is unproven.

However, in a path-breaking paper titled 'The Real Failure Rate of Restaurants', Cornell University's Chris Muller and Michigan State University's Robert H. Woods proved that the actual failure rates observed for three different markets in the US over 10 years were much lower than the anecdotal 90 per cent. The real rate, according to Muller and Woods, was about 60 per cent at the end of five years of operation.

Of course, this study cannot simply be extrapolated to India, but it proves one point: to take the 90 per cent figure with a pinch of salt.

From my own observation of tracking restaurants for so long, however, I can tell you how a majority of them that open with a bang *do* end with a whimper. Many linger on for a variety of reasons for longer than fiscally prudent: because of owner/chef vanities, because of rent clauses that lock in tenants from moving out before a few years, and because even when tenants default on rent, landlords often dread the long legal process to evict them.

Restaurant failures can be very hard to define and spot because, as we have said, many simply change names, interiors and themes and open as brand-new bars or restaurants sometimes even before the first full year is complete. There are also those that limp on for much longer, running in losses, before the owners run out of funds, lose all hope and finally shut, never to be heard of again.

In an *Economic Times* article in 2017,[9] Riyaaz Amlani, then president of the NRAI, was quoted as saying, 'The conditions are tough and the regulatory environment is very complicated. If you see any of these best restaurant lists from a year like 2010, out of 20 of them, 15 do not exist any more.'

Suffice to say, any first-time restaurant needs to be cautious rather than rush in. However, here we must ask ourselves what exactly it is that we call failure or success in this business.

Do bars that run for two years and then try to revamp constitute success (even if they have recovered their investment and made a profit)? Or is the longevity of a brand important? In that case, are long-standing restaurants that get only 60 per cent full even on weekends successful? What about critically acclaimed and chef-led restaurants that may be running only because of 'friendly investments' (like old-fashioned patronage to artists), without making adequate profits, ploughing back all that is earned into PR and marketing, or even being subsidized by allied businesses? What of restaurateurs and hoteliers who say one of their restaurants is to 'make a name' while others make money and sustain that super brand? (This is more common in restaurants that do not pay rent. While restaurant revenue is more and more important to hotels in India today, some restaurants within hotels function as brand-building exercises, pegged in a luxury segment, which sees fewer customers than affordable or premium casual dining standalones.)

Most studies that delve into failure rates of restaurants

look at these from a purely financial point of view and from data on bankrupt companies (in other countries). However, any definition of success or failure must depend on what the original intent of the restaurateur was.

Profit cannot be the only definition of success when you are running an establishment where the idea is to treat food as art, where rigorous experimentation is aided by six-monthly R&D breaks for the staff (as in the case of top restaurants in the world such as Noma, or several restaurants in San Sebastian, Spain's restaurant capital). Restaurants such as these do not seem to solely look at food costs – which are naturally very high, as are the wage bills. They have diners fly in from all over the world to splurge on a single meal, they have expensive wines that they are able to sell to rich diners in substantial quantities and they obviously make money.

However, with high costs, including the cost of those long research breaks and astronomical PR and marketing expenses, which keeps them on influential lists such as the World's 50 Best, what profits are their promoters actually making? That is not clear.

What is clear though is that at this highest level, profit is not the only motive for running these restaurants. Instead, the creative hubris of the chef and prestige for partners in the business are motivations. In these world's top restaurants, the chefs as celebrities do make quite a career for themselves, and there may be spin-off offers, endorsements, TV or Netflix shows that enable them to monetize their celebrity status, but it is arguable how much profit the restaurant per se makes after the heavy expenses.

We need to remember though that these are exceptional, exclusive luxury restaurants, of the kind that we do not have in India yet primarily because the market for luxury dining is very small. We shall discuss this theme too later in the book.

However, a restaurant like Masque in Mumbai, three years old, where chef Prateek Sadhu has been pushing the envelope of kitchen creativity, is an example of a restaurant run for other reasons than profit. Sadhu, who re-examines his Kashmiri heritage through food – by cooking inspired dishes treated in a modernist way – began with a focus on pan-Indian seasonal ingredients at Masque, located in an offbeat, not easy to access mill compound in Mumbai. The restaurant offers only a tasting menu to diners, which is not even printed but only verbally communicated to them.

Once a diner sits down, there are different courses of food treated in unexpected ways that may not necessarily earn the adjective 'delicious' but, like art, make a diner sit up and think. Diners eat what the chef chooses and also get a tour of the experimental kitchen between courses.

This is not populist dining, it is avant garde work. Masque gets expats and tourists, but few local Mumbai diners. In the initial six months, Sadhu told me he would sometimes get just two tables on a weekend.

Yet, he and the restaurant's valiant owner Aditi Dugar have ploughed on, trying to create cuisine as art. Financially, it may be making nowhere close to the ₹1.5-crore-a-month sales that some buzzing bars in Delhi and Mumbai claim to do – in fact, I don't see how it is making much profit at all; however, as an artistic enterprise, and as a thought leader in the Indian gastronomic space, Masque is successful.

For most restaurateurs in India, though, success is a mix of both (i) the brand, the quality it represents and longevity; and (ii) profitability. Even Indian Accent – our only representative on the Asia's 50 Best list, the poster child of modern Indian food and one of the few fine-dining restaurants in the country – looks at food costs and profit margins strictly because it needs to survive as an enterprise in a tough business environment.

People who are not looking to be artists or patrons, those who are not vanity investors or looking to gain social equity even if their business makes no profit, must enter the restaurant business with caution and prudence. Money launderers, socialites and gig-to-gig jumpers may see restaurants as short-term businesses which you can cash out of after a year or two and they may all have good reasons for wanting to be restaurateurs. But if you are a more serious novice entrepreneur who wants to build quality restaurant brands even as you make fair money, read on.

Why do so many restaurants fail?

Restaurant failure is often described as something mysterious. You will find many failed restaurateurs who will tell you that they had set up a really good restaurant and yet it failed for inexplicable reasons, that there were simply not enough customers. These sorts of statements point to a lack of insight. There are a surprising number of common reasons for restaurant failure that owners are sometimes unable to spot. Some of these mistakes, such as an inexperienced restaurateur starting out with less funds than necessary and not accounting for various extras like project delays that are inevitable in the Indian scenario, are evident and can be avoided by doing due diligence and speaking to established restaurateurs who are open with their advice these days. Then there are other common reasons like partners falling out, which no one can do anything about – like for any business, you need to choose your partners and team well, but these are individual decisions. However, there are a few other key factors that are often not understood by many restaurateurs. Let's look at these closely.

Lack of clarity about the product and food

Is the food and restaurant concept 'authentic', unique or a copy? What is your story and does your food have one? Who is your audience and how are you going to price the food so that it is good value for that audience (because every audience in India does want value for money, and even if the restaurant is expensive, the audience needs to find value in it)? As an aspiring restaurateur, these are some of the first questions you need to address.

Many established restaurateurs begin by first seeking out a suitable space or location for a restaurant and then deciding which concept to 'fit' into it. In my opinion, while some people may indeed have a gift for this and be able to connect with markets alien to them after some research (Camellia Panjabi spent a whole year in London before starting the Taj's restaurant there, she told me), this may not be an ideal approach.

When established restaurateurs with multiple outlets seize upon a location first even before they know what they are going to do with it, it is a reflection of the fact that good real estate for restaurants is so hard to come by in the metros; when prestigious new real estate projects come up, there is naturally competition within the industry to get the best spots.

For a first-time restaurateur, however, this approach is not right and likely to fail in the long run. If you are interested in creating a brand with longevity, you need to think about what it is that you want to serve. This does not mean that you only think about the kind of food you would like to offer, but in fact what the entire product will be, what it will feel like – in other words the 'tonality' of it. Is it going to be young and casual? Or more upscale and sophisticated? And so on. In keeping with what kind of a product you will build and for what kind of an audience, you will then need to determine what kind of food it will serve, which is, obviously, no less important. If you are a chef or home cook who is getting into the business, you would obviously have thought about the food first: what your approach to food is and what it is that you specifically want to feed your customers. But even if you are just a restaurateur with no strong opinion or passion for a particular kind of food, you still need to zero in on a cuisine that you – or your team – have some synergy with, that you identify with.

After you have figured out a rough idea for the food and the concept, you need to go location scouting. Once you have a location in mind, you need to examine the market, check out the competition and figure out the gap. You need to study your potential audience, determine how best what you are offering will suit your customers, tailor your product according to this and determine the price people are likely to be comfortable paying.

This, I firmly believe, is the correct approach any first-time restaurateur should adopt. It has been followed by some of the best, most successful restaurant brands started by newcomers.

For instance, when Italian ex-banker Oscar Balcon opened Artusi in 2014 in Delhi's Greater Kailash II, just a stone's throw away from Diva, the definitive Italian restaurant in India, food circles were abuzz with the kind of research he had already done and the clarity of thought he possessed.

First, instead of generic Italian food, Balcon and his wife (partners in the business) knew that they would focus on specials from the region of Emilia Romagnia, where Balcon's family comes from, and that they therefore know best. Instead of a generic pizza–pasta restaurant – the only kind of 'Italian' middle-class Indians are deemed to know – the restaurant would serve high-quality regional Italian food. This much was clear to the first-time entrepreneurs.

Being firm about their concept and not willing to dilute it to please all had its advantages and limitations. Balcon and his wife knew that because the market for such speciality dinning was limited, their restaurant would have to be small and target a select, more sophisticated audience. This at once differentiated it from the usual cafes in this space. And of course, the size of the audience and the fact that the ingredients for such food are hard to find also meant that the restaurant would have to be upscale and relatively expensive.

Knowing decisively what they wanted to serve made all these things immediately clear.

Then the couple got a chef and a manager on board – key members of the team intrinsic to the experience being offered. It was only after the core team was formed that they went location hunting for a 'small place with a good landlord', as Balcon told me. They zeroed in on GK II, in the belief that affluent residents in the neighbourhood would provide clientele. But in hindsight, Balcon told me, he feels that a speciality restaurant like theirs would have drawn its niche audience even at another location.

Before they started operations, the restaurateur knew his product and its strengths and limitations as well as the competition in the cluttered market in which he would be playing. Finally, he was also clear in how his offering was different from Diva's, the market leader in the category, located just a few stores down the lane from the new restaurant. (Artusi began with offering regional Italian food. Its menu is quite different from Diva's.)

Artusi in GK II was a success. Meanwhile, many other Italian restaurants trying to serve Italian food have not made the cut, including local players in the same market and international ones like Jamie's Italian, which came in as a big-bang foreign brand opening. The difference between all these other restaurants and Artusi is that the latter is a sharply defined product targeted at a sharply defined audience – something that can only happen when the restaurateur has clarity right from the beginning.

Meanwhile, Mumbai's Bombay Canteen, a case study in how to launch a successful restaurant, is another example of a business that knew its business much before it started.

The Bombay Canteen opened in February 2015 with three co-founders: Sameer Seth, Yash Bhanage and chef Floyd Cardoz. Seth and Bhanage, who had studied hospitality management together in the US, had been mentored by Cardoz at his New York restaurant, and this core team, already committed to each other, was also committed to the idea of launching a modern Indian restaurant in India – given Cardoz's expertise with the cuisine he had successfully sold at Danny Meyer's Tabla in New York.

With Cardoz as a partner, it was evident right from the beginning that the food would be the kind that the chef has been known for in New York – modern Indian but based on regional recipes, in particular drawing from Cardoz's own childhood memories. To fine-tune this intended product and suss out the competition not just in Mumbai but nationally, the team went on a research and dining mission across the metros.

(As an aside, in mid-2014, as I sat trying out another kind of modern Indian food being served by the newly opened Farzi Café at Gurugram's Cyber Hub, a restaurant that relied on quirky presentation of classic Indian dishes, I spotted the Bombay Canteen promoters dining quietly at a table in the new restaurant. No doubt part of their research drive.)

No one knew them and they possibly found out everything that they had hoped to. This painstaking research about their competition and consumer behaviour when it came to modern Indian food across the metros obviously helped them crystallize their thoughts and refine their concept.

Few restaurateurs are as meticulous. Most suffer because of their lack of clarity about the kind of food or drink experience they are going to serve and because they don't clearly understand the kind of potential audience that will attract. There are too many examples all around us of a restaurant that is doomed to fail because the owners are blindly copying a concept or making a patchwork of ideas and cuisines in a space that may look stunning and is expensively designed but has no soul because there is no vision in place.

With stiff competition in markets that are oversupplied

by similar restaurants and bars, price becomes the only differentiating factor to draw in customers and undercutting follows. A new restaurant naturally suffers in such a scenario. Which is why a new restaurant must be unique, well conceptualized and sufficiently differentiated from its rivals.

Lack of financial clarity

A lot of restaurants fail because restaurateurs, especially first-time restaurateurs who are funding their own ventures, have rushed into the business without assessing the full financial requirements and risks. While costs at different locations vary widely even in the same city or micro-market, in general, it is entirely possible to spend a capex of around ₹3 crore for a premium casual diner. Chef and restaurateur Manu Chandra points out that this, however, is only the beginning. 'By the time you are ready to open three to six months down the line because there are inevitable delays, you realize you are another ₹50 lakh down. Then there are marketing spends of another ₹20–30 lakh. So even before you have opened, you realize you are ₹4 crore down. This obviously puts a lot of pressure on a new entrepreneur, and the way you do business gets invariably impacted.' With so much money at stake, an individual restaurateur obviously is under a lot of stress to recover it fast.

To recover capex may take between 18 months to three years, depending on the format of the bar or restaurant, according to various restaurateurs. Operational break-even should happen much faster, within six months to one year usually, but even if you are operationally breaking even, you must have the capacity to be able to wait patiently for your money. There are astounding success stories I hear about some bars where the capex has been recovered in under a year and operational break-even from the very beginning of operations. However, these are exceptions and not the rule. As a first-time restaurateur, you must ignore them.

A lot of glamour-struck restaurateurs land up spending unnecessary money on how the restaurant looks, on fancy kitchen equipment that may not be needed, because without a proper understanding of how a kitchen works, they have been misguided by consultants and so on.

If you don't have money to burn, think like a middle-class housewife and be frugal. At the end of the day, what you are putting on the table will always matter more to customers than how your restaurant looks. It is also very hard to fill up very big restaurants and no one wants to go into half-empty restaurants – so do not be taken in by deals on very large spaces. On the other hand, small restaurants that are less than 30 to 40 covers, or seats, may never earn enough money to make it worthwhile. So you need an optimum size at a smart rent and then you need to be smart about how much you are spending on renovation per square foot, on the kitchen and so on. However, the flip side is that large-format bars and restaurants have a greater potential to make money – provided you know how to earn optimally from every square foot of the space. A new restaurateur may want to start not with a 100-seater but perhaps with a reasonable 60- to 70-seater.

You need to figure out your projected earnings. As a conservative restaurateur running a food-led restaurant, or where food makes up at least 50 per cent of the sales, rent should not be more than 20 per cent of your revenue. Salaries these days are not cheap but should not be more than 20 per cent, food cost should not be more than 30–35 per cent, and utilities and extras should account for another 5–6 per cent. If you manage such strict figures, your resulting store-level profit will be deemed quite good. In reality, this does not always fall into place quite so seamlessly. Rents are higher in marquee locations, food cost can run amok, and policy changes such as GST can impact calculations. I spoke to Sharad Sachdeva, former CEO of the Amit Burman–promoted restaurant company Lite Bite Foods, who now heads operations of L Catterton, the private equity arm of French conglomerate LVMH. According to him, if the store-level EBITDA of a restaurant is over 20 per cent, it is doing exceptionally well; if it is 15–20 per cent, it is good; if it's 10–15 per cent, it is average; and less than 10 per cent is poor. Very few experience-led restaurants in India are doing exceptional or even good or average business, as per this criterion, according to many restaurateurs I spoke to in private. Internationally, many consultants use some formulae for the first year of a new restaurant's operations, when costs, especially food, are going to be higher and a restaurateur will still be figuring out customer flow, ordering and scheduling. Whatever you are using, you must account for several extras as well, in particular for project delays that inevitably dog restaurateuring in India.

Ashish's theory of the clock

Sometimes, restaurants fail because they are either too ahead or behind their 'time'. In hindsight, we can all spot the ones that came up before their intended audience was ready for the cuisine or idea they were serving up. Others arrived at the fag end of a trend when the public was already bored of that particular 'theme'. Molecular gastronomy is a case in point. It's a 'trend' that has lived its day. El Bulli's Ferran Adria, considered to be one of the greatest innovators of this century and the father of everything from spherification to foams, didn't quite think of molecular gastronomy as a cuisine in its own right.

From the mid-1980s, when Adria joined El Bulli, through the mid-1990s, when it started attracting the attention of wealthy diners, through the early 2000s (it became number one on the World's 50 Best Restaurants list in 2002), the chef's idea was to present Spanish dishes in new ways while keeping their essence intact. In fact, Adria did not even consider his cuisine to be 'molecular gastronomy', the term it was associated with later. In the hands of lesser copycat chefs, molecular gastronomy became an end in itself. Chef after chef landed up copying its tropes, such as foams and air, without necessarily managing to retain the essence of whatever they were deconstructing or dishing up. The whole genre became pastiche. Inevitably, diners became wary of soulless experimentation, which has now had its day.

El Bulli shut in 2011. Adria has been hosting exhibitions, working with big companies and setting up a foundation that promotes innovation. Yet there are restaurants in Kolkata or Chennai or Gurugram that seek to badly copy his kind of kitchen chemistry through cheaply bought kits now available online. These pastiche restaurants obviously are destined to fail. They came to the party too late and the public – even in the mid-market segment in India – is bored of those plates.

It's a similar case with co-working spaces within restaurants. The idea was unique when Social, Riyaaz Amlani's brand, first unveiled it to millennial consumers in 2014. Five years down the line, every failed or confused restaurant, bar or cafe wants to be a co-working space too. Amlani showed that the model could succeed with millennials because they identified with it, and the co-working concept ensured a steady clientele throughout the day, instead of having to depend on just the weekend bar crawlers. Today, there are start-ups that offer to convert your cafe or bar into a co-working space and manage these, and existing restaurants wanting to convert their brand offering to 'co-working' from whatever they were. It is my contention that these will not really work. The novelty has worn off and there are too many people with similar offerings in the market, making it impossible for a new brand to establish some sort of customer loyalty, which is vital to running such a concept dependent on people coming to it month after month, paying a small fixed deposit redeemable against food, and sitting and working from the space.

Sometimes, on the other hand, restaurants seem to come up ahead of their time. Though thanks to travel and the Internet, customers in India are far more accepting of a wide variety of cuisines and ideas than ever before, and cities like Mumbai in particular are welcoming of new concepts, many markets are still conservative. The acceptance for Indian (and modern Indian) food with its bold flavours and familiar tastes is still far higher than for any other cuisine. Japanese, Korean, Sri Lankan, Mexican and so on exist, but only in pockets. Then there are other cuisines that are trendy in other global dining capitals such as Spanish or Peruvian, which do not even make an appearance in the Indian restaurant-scape. Even cuisines from within the country – from the north-east, from states like Odisha or even Bengal – are not widespread enough in the mass market in most cities, including Delhi and Mumbai, the two food capitals of India.

The mass audience may not be ready for concepts centred on a single specialized cuisine, though some of these restaurants may work at a niche level. However, with our restaurant culture steadily evolving, there may be a time in the near future when these restaurants become acceptable to a wider section of the public, perhaps even a majority.

Restaurateur Ashish Kapur, who owns brands such as The Wine Company, Whisky Samba and Antares in Delhi, Mumbai and Goa, told me that he advises wannabe restaurateurs on how important it is to be 'just five minutes ahead of the clock'.

He means a metaphoric clock ticking away with every change in popular culture and consumer tastes. What Kapur underscores is the importance of timing while opening restaurants with themes or speciality cuisines; the same also holds for bars such as his that focus on specifics (wine and whisky in his case).

Before The Wine Company opened in Gurugram in 2014, there really wasn't a bar dedicated to wine – though many bars, especially in Mumbai, where the number of wine drinkers was deemed to be far greater than in Scotch country NCR, had great wine lists. This was both because of the lack of international wine labels at reasonable prices, as well as the fact that the Punjabi palate thought as being the driver for restaurant business in much of India preferred 'macho' drinks like whisky or beer to wine. India had no wine culture – and few Indian wines of an acceptable quality were being produced.

Five years ago, all this started to change. More women started drinking and a newer generation started taking to wine not as an occasional drink to impress an expat boss but as part of a more global lifestyle in which you could socialize over a glass that didn't have to cost a fortune. This was organic social evolution. While India still has punishing import duties on wine, making many international labels that are drinkable and reasonably priced in their home markets inaccessible in the country, younger importers started getting in experimental and easy-to-drink New World labels, while small domestic wineries like Krsma and York started making some good wine. The Wine Company launched at exactly such a time when both consumer habits were changing and more exciting wine was becoming available, and it became a market leader. It was five minutes ahead of the clock.

The metaphorical clock is a measure of changing public attitudes, tastes and pop culture. A restaurateur must be just a little ahead of the clock for their restaurant to click and become a trendsetter. The catch, of course, is: how does a restaurateur time their offerings? Popular tastes and culture are rapidly changing, and to predict how things will pan out is difficult. However, if you are in touch with the pop culture of the day, you may be quickly able to sense how things are moving. That is why the truth about restaurateuring, which applies to many businesses, is that it is about personal instinct. At the end of the day, this is a business about people – for the people, by the people. The personality of a restaurateur, their instinct and how clued in they are with the pop culture of their market are those intangibles that permeate the business. We will study these factors in the second part of the book, in which I will elaborate on my own theory of how successful restaurateurs put a bit of themselves in their brands.

What makes a restaurant successful?

How does an entrepreneur cook up a successful restaurant? As with the most inspired Indian dishes, there isn't really any recipe – there is only *andaz*, an approximation of quantities based on individual perception, of the many ingredients that make for a restaurant's success. All the ingredients must come together. If one thing goes off, it has the potential to ruin the whole.

Location, location, location

Many people in the business routinely peg location as the most important ingredient in determining a restaurant's success. Location is, of course, of vital importance. If a restaurant is located in a spot with a good catchment area for prospective consumers, it is obviously a big advantage. But how advantageous a location will be for a particular restaurant in proportion to the rent you are paying can be hard to gauge. A marquee location comes at a certain price. If you are renting a property in premium locations like Delhi's Khan Market or Mumbai's BKC or in an upcoming mall by a reputed company, in which all the big restaurant companies are investing, the rent that you pay and the terms that you accept are going to be stiff. A new restaurant may not have that kind of money or enough clout to negotiate better terms.

Though a good location is important and there are

many examples of restaurants failing because of locations that turned out to be bad, not attracting the right kind of audience or enough of an audience for a concept, it is not a given that a supposedly advantageous location, one that is deemed premium, equals financial success for any restaurant. There are many examples of restaurants in the metros that seemingly chose good locations but never achieved success. At the end of the day, restaurateuring is about a fine balance – many things must come together in sync for a restaurant to be a success.

Instead, of thinking about 'good' locations, restaurateurs may ponder about 'appropriate' locations for their specific concepts. Very often, restaurateurs are not able to assess the advantage or disadvantage of a location in advance. Delhi's Meherchand Market for years had been touted as the next Khan Market – one of the most expensive retail markets in India – by those within the industry. Several restaurants opened here on that premise that the location would develop like Khan Market and start attracting the same kind of evolved and higher-spending clientele – and shut. Meherchand Market, though it was located centrally and surrounded by posh residential neighbourhoods, never graduated into a prime restaurant hub. Those who suffered as a result were Vimi and K.D. Singh, a couple (she was a designer, he was a pilot) who had decided to launch their passion project here. They sunk in a total of ₹1 crore into a charming little restaurant that, as Vimi told me, offered reasonably good, home-style continental food that KD supervised personally, but ended up putting in ₹1 lakh every month out of their pockets to meet expenses. It was a year and a half before they decided that enough was enough and the location was not working. The restaurant finally closed down. I can think of no other reason for that but a poor location that just did not attract enough customers.

Could the restaurant have fared better in a busier retail zone like the neighbouring Khan Market? Possibly. However, a busier and better-established restaurant hub would entail higher rents and also more competition. Locales like Khan Market in Delhi, Cyber Hub in Gurugram, and Kamala Mills and BKC in Mumbai obviously charge higher rents than many other high-street or mall locations.

There are three things to keep in mind: A new location, even by a good developer will always be a risk, even if you hear about other prominent restaurant companies investing there – we don't quite know how it will work for a restaurant, though a restaurateur can make an informed guess. If you have deep pockets and are risk-averse, you may want to look for space in a prime, established hub. Finally, even in prime locations, not all restaurants are successful.

Location is important. But it is for a restaurateur to decide whether their product is strong or distinctive enough to come up in an offbeat place, take advantage of a lower rent and still pull in customers. It's a high-risk strategy and works only if you know very clearly what your product is and who you are catering to. A speciality or chef-led restaurant that caters to a more upscale crowd has a better chance of becoming a 'destination restaurant' than an average or generic-seeming restaurant.

There are quite a few examples of restaurants that have proved to be successful while working with a perceived locational disadvantage. Indian Accent, India's most famous restaurant today, is an excellent example of how an offbeat location – in the middle of a residential colony, not frequented by anyone seeking any retail experience – worked for a restaurant that aimed to push boundaries and tread new ground when it opened in 2009 in the leafy Friends Colony enclave of New Delhi.

What worked for the restaurant was the rent advantage it got from such a low-key location. Most people in the industry, and many outside it, are aware that Indian Accent was not financially successful from day one. In fact, it hung in there by a thread for several years, not making enough money even though it was always critically acclaimed.

Modern Indian as a cuisine was new to India and the market for it developed slowly. It was only three to four years down the line that Indian Accent became so popular that it was impossible to find a table without reserving weeks in advance. Rental costs were negligible because Indian Accent's parent company, Old World Hospitality, had the licence for running The Manor, the boutique hotel where the restaurant opened and ran, before shifting to its present location at The Lodhi in 2017. So it did not have to pay the rent the area would have otherwise commanded, and the restaurant was able to pull on for several years even if it did not earn too much money. Had an experimental concept such as this opened in a marquee location with high rents, it would almost certainly have had to shut without having enough time to develop into a super successful brand.

When The Bombay Canteen opened in 2015 in the 37-acre premises of Mumbai's Kamala Mills area, till then a desultory compound not boasting of much restaurant retail, nobody was sure of the business it would get, including its owners, who were first-time restaurateurs. 'Because of the offices around, we thought we would get lunch business but we didn't know whether we would get a dinner crowd. So, we really focused on our dinners initially,' says co-founder Sameer Seth.

The 'destination' restaurant proved to be successful because of many factors – there was a gap for casual Indian food in Mumbai (unlike in, say, Delhi-NCR, where many more restaurants with all sorts of Indian cuisines existed), the vibe TBC created was attractive to the cosmopolitan and even 'woke millennial' audience of the area around Lower Parel, the bar and food quality was high and presentations chic but not traditional or gimmicky, and the marketing and PR was definitely above average and a key to establishing the brand. The success in fact turned Kamala Mills into the country's leading food hub within just two years of its opening. Till a fire at the end of 2017 in one of the restaurants in the complex claimed many lives and drove away the crowds, and before BKC took over as a prime restaurant hub, Kamala Mills was the hottest destination for restaurants. Many upcoming restaurants sought it out in the hope of getting a ready-made crowd; some did well, while others didn't as oversupply started eating into business, but all the newcomers had to pay much higher rents than The Bombay Canteen.

Setting up a restaurant in an offbeat location that does not get walk-in customers is obviously a risk. But it has a potential to reap rich rewards. At Kamala Mills, rents doubled from ₹200 per sq. ft to ₹400 per sq. ft in less than two years (most restaurants there operate on a model of a certain fixed rent plus revenue share, a practice many other landlords follow in India). As a first mover, The Bombay Canteen benefited from having negotiated a better deal than others who came in later. In a low-margin business, that can be the difference between success and failure – if the restaurant concept is strong enough to pull in the crowds.

The cliché about 'good food'

Most people think that good food is another key ingredient for the success of any restaurant. But this idea is problematic because the definition of good food is highly subjective. And then there are many restaurants that seem to do quite well financially even though their food is popularly and critically deemed to be just average, not superlative.

Sometimes, the food is even less than 'average'.

Good food must always be viewed within a context. If it is a speciality restaurant where customer expectation is built around exceptional cooking or unique cuisines, the restaurant must deliver. However, if it is a casual multi-cuisine restaurant, a bar, a cafe or a dhaba, the definition of good food changes. Parameters used for a fine-dining or chef-led restaurant are not applicable. A customer is happy when they think they are getting food at a quality that they perceive as value for their money. A portion of precisely cooked black cod for ₹3,500 may be just as good value as an aloo tikki burger for ₹35, or spicy pink pasta for ₹150 in Agra, when the restaurant experience changes. (However, on the other hand, if you are a restaurant that is communicating a certain high quality of experience to its audience, obviously badly made chaat, less nuanced than the street vendor outside, or Manchurian, even if cleverly plated, are going to fall flat because the customer will find no exclusivity for the price and promise.)

It is important for restaurants to serve food in sync with what they are promising to customers verbally and implicitly. A restaurant also has to be consistent about this brand promise via the quality of food that it is serving. Food quality cannot vary every day. In India, restaurants survive on repeat clientele and if food quality is not consistent, a restaurant starts losing its clientele. People come into a certain restaurant with a certain set of expectations; the moment these are not fulfilled, they leave. In the restaurant business, the biggest loss is of customers who come in and never return after a less-than-satisfactory experience – people who disappear without even leaving any feedback.

The X factor: Personality on a platter

What makes a restaurant successful is obviously the entire product – which includes everything from food, design and service to experience, pricing and concept. The product needs to be relevant to the particular market it is competing in. To arrive at the right product is clearly quite difficult, otherwise we would have had many more successful restaurants. The process of everything falling into place can seem almost alchemical at times. As a reviewer, I find that I can sense almost from the moment I walk into a space whether it will click or not. It is perhaps being able to sense whether a product has come together coherently or not, whether there are any incongruous or discordant notes that will ruin it.

Many old hands in the business, like restaurateur Marut Sikka, call this a restaurant's 'X factor'. (Many years ago while talking to me, he tried to give a formula for getting this X factor right: 80 per cent good food, 20 per cent good service and ambience, while excelling in at least one category, so that customers go back feeling that at least one of the three components – food, service or ambience – is excellent.) Restaurateur Riyaaz Amlani calls it a restaurant's 'tonality', that quality that you know is in tune with the intended audience. If a restaurant is *besur*, out of tune, you know it.

In the absence of any magical recipe, how does one achieve this perfect harmony, this X factor, this coming together of the various elements of a restaurant pitched to the 'right' audience?

After having studied many restaurants over the years, it is my belief that the oft-touted X factor is only a function of a restaurateur's own personality. This is true for restaurants that seek to create an experience and are not merely functional. When the personality of a restaurateur is in sync with their product and with their intended audience, magic happens. Very often, the most successful restaurateurs and chefs are those who serve up little bits of themselves, their beliefs, lifestyle and intrinsic nature or values on the platter. This is my belief born out of close observation. The public perhaps has an instinct to latch on to this elusive and hard-to-define quality, which nevertheless comes through in the consumer's experience. This is truly the most important ingredient for a restaurant's success and we will study this in greater detail in the next chapter, in which I analyse just how the country's most successful restaurateurs have put little bits of their personality into their brands.

Chain businesses and QSRs are different. These are systems-led. We will talk about them later in the book. But even these do reflect certain subliminal values or culture as part of their brand – even a sanitized McDonald's does. Standalone, experience-led restaurants need to be personalized. They only work when a restaurateur or chef who is the captain of the ship is consistently involved in the business, ideating, conceptualizing, monitoring, correcting and micromanaging. This close involvement is vital. Unless a restaurateur knows their audience well and has an understanding of the subculture the customers belong to even within the same city, they cannot pitch their product right and cannot correct things promptly.

For this to happen, a restaurateur or chef must intimately know what they are serving and communicating and to whom. Somebody trying to do a South American restaurant in Delhi when they have no intimate connection with that cuisine or culture and do not intrinsically understand the niche, cosmopolitan audience that such a restaurant needs in a country like India cannot hope to succeed. Even if a restaurateur knows the food they are serving well but has no connection with the audience they are serving it to, they cannot succeed. It is for this reason that passion projects sometimes fail. An authentic Mangalorean restaurant started by a home cook with the best ghee roast this side of the Deccan cannot work in Karol Bagh if the chef/restaurateur cannot work the audience.

Restaurants that are in sync with their owner's personalities are ultimately successful because both the product and the potential audience are instinctively understood at a subliminal level by the restaurateur. As you will see in Part 2, if you analyse restaurateur A.D. Singh and Olive, his flagship brand, you can see how this works. Riyaaz Amlani takes great care to hang out with younger people and told me that he fears missing out on contemporary culture with all its nuances; Social, his brand, is built on the premise of being a unique space for younger consumers, even as each of the outlets are customized to cater to different subcultures of consumers in different locations. There is a lot of detailing involved instead of it being a generic restaurant catering to a general 'millennial' audience. Before Amlani started the first Social in Bengaluru, he spent considerable time in the city understanding its specific vibe. The consumers in central Delhi are different from those in south Delhi, which are different from those in Mumbai suburbs or town, which are different from those in Bengaluru, Pune and Hyderabad, even if they do share many similarities in aspirations and what they connect with thanks to a common youth culture spawned by the internet, films, sport and so on. The brand taps into both the similarities and differences by having the same DNA but tuning into specifics as it goes from one place to another, because of Amlani's personal engagement with culture. Restaurateur Zorawar Kalra's ambition is to be the biggest and the best and this aspiration is subliminally felt in all his restaurants – and also tellingly in the name of his company, Massive Restaurants.

If we take this argument to its logical conclusion, we will see why copycat projects often flounder. You cannot run a 'cool' bar if you yourself are conservative, old-school and fuddy-duddy. (Teetotallers are known to run very successful bars – like Vaibhav Singh of Perch in Delhi – but we are talking about personalities and attitudes not personal habits and preferences.) We will dwell in greater detail on this theory of mine as we study the personalities of various restaurateurs whom I have had the pleasure of observing at length, and being friends with, and how these personalities have shaped their restaurants.

PART 2

3

A PLATEFUL OF PERSONALITY

Of all the factors behind a successful brand, one that is crucial, yet perhaps least understood, is the restaurateur's personality. The mysterious 'X factor' that people talk about when they talk about successful and distinctive restaurant brands. This is much like a popular person's or even a film star's charisma and is about how a restaurant connects almost intuitively with its intended audience in a unique fit.

Most people are not able to put a finger on this. What is this alchemy by which all the things that go into the making of a restaurant's unique 'personality' or 'character' – from concept and location to food and service – fall into place, creating a 'vibe' that is different from any other in the market?

This 'personality' or vibe of the restaurant is much more than the look and feel of the space, and it positively resonates with the personality of the customer base in a successful restaurant brand. Basically, this is nothing but the essence of a restaurateur's core values that are always present in any brand and subliminally sensed by customers. The most successful restaurateurs are those who are conscious of who they really are, are able to distil their essence and communicate it successfully both within the company and externally. As customers, we sense this personality communicated to us in various ways – through the look and feel, service, style and the kind of food on offer, but also as something more than the sum of all these.

This essence that we subliminally sense may or may not draw us in, depending on who we are as people and what we value. But we are able to sense this as we enter a restaurant space.

We are not talking about chains – which may be QSRs or others serving basic food. These operations that require scale become systems-led as they grow and may not be reflections of any one restaurateur's personality or values. It may still be possible to argue that even McDonald's, founded by the brothers Richard and Maurice 'Mac' McDonald, is a reflection of a certain set of cultural values or ideas of America, or that the numerous Udupi chains in India reflect the cultural values of the frugal Udupi brahmins. However, this book is devoted to 'experience-led' restaurants, whether 'premium', 'casual' or 'luxury', and for most of these restaurants success reflects the values, ethos or personality of their owners.

Restaurants have personalities that reflect their owners'

because these are highly individualistic businesses, constantly needing a human touch, and the most successful ones are businesses that have been created out of a sense of passion. Much like other 'arty' retail businesses that offer an 'experience', restaurants need an emotional connect with their consumers – something that happens when the restaurateur's personality is in sync both with what they are offering and with the subculture of their intended audience.

Take Kwality, a restaurant with a heritage that spans almost 80 years (it was one of the first restaurants to come up in Lutyens' Delhi in 1940,[1] just around the time of World War II. The owners can easily earn ₹15 lakh a month in rental income, according to my rough calculations, if they sit back and simply let out their prime, central Delhi property.

Yet Sunil Lamba and his sons Dhruv and Divij choose to continue to run the restaurant that was set up by Sunil's father P.L. Lamba before Partition. The Lambas have recently, in 2019, invested a considerable amount of money in completely revamping Kwality's old premises.

After a seven-month refurbishing, a shiny new-yet-old space has opened with a vintage chandelier and piano, Villeroy and Boch crockery, leather upholstery for the couches, old photographs of central Delhi sourced from the iconic studio Mahatta & Co., and so on. When this investment will be recouped remains to be seen. Kwality, with its pedigree, old-style Continental and Punjabi food and vintage colonial air, stands in Connaught Place, a central business district which has lost its sheen, is no longer frequented by the elite and instead is the hub of a nouveau, young crowd that frequents the many new 'buzzing' bars that sell cheap alcohol and chatpata and low-brow Indian food by and large. Kwality's laidback charm and the nostalgia it evokes, in fact, are contrary to the dominant eating-out culture in Connaught Place today.

The restaurant cannot thus hope to depend on casual walk-ins, as per my analysis. Instead, it needs to recreate itself as a dining destination for people from all over the city, when they want to dine on hearty, old-school food with an air of the vintage. This task is going to be tough in a competitive market despite the considerable equity the brand enjoys and despite so many families that have an emotional connect with it – including mine (my parents met over coffee there and the family continues to be big fans of the restaurant's iconic dish, chole bhature). After all, many millennial customers, who spend at restaurants and bars in general more frequently, may not have the same nostalgia for Kwality as an older generation of customers, who are occasional consumers and come in less frequently. Also, within such a cluttered market as Connaught Place, full of bars and eateries, there seems to be an oversupply of restaurants, which obviously impacts everyone's business.

The Lambas have their work cut out to make their restaurant work and earn enough. To make ₹15 lakh in profit (the equivalent of rental income) every month, the refurbished restaurant will need to earn a monthly revenue of close to ₹0.75–1 crore (store EBITDA calculated as 15–20 per cent of restaurant revenue as per industry norms for well-run restaurants, as discussed in Part 1). This is difficult for a mid-priced restaurant focused on food rather than alcohol. To recoup the investment made to spruce up the legacy, the family will have to wait longer. These are calculations based on standard operations of restaurants within India – if everything goes right. There's always the risk that plans fail.

When you see the blood, sweat and tears a restaurateur puts into the business, you realize it isn't all that much about money. Profit cannot be your sole motive for opening a restaurant. But profit is necessary to be able to run one.

For the Lambas, it is about emotions linked to the family. 'Our father's heart and spirit still reside here,' says Timma Lamba, Sunil Lamba's wife, when I meet her for lunch one day at Kwality and she goes over the story of how it all started.

Pishori Lal Lamba had come to Delhi in 1940, seven years before Partition, with few prospects and fewer means other than his sharp mind. He started out by selling hand-cranked ice cream to American troops posted in the British Indian capital around World War II. The soldiers would come to eat this after late-night film shows at Regal Cinema, and Lamba's modest enterprise became successful.

It was an American soldier posted in Delhi who had advised P.L. Lamba to serve ice cream late in the night to get customers who would watch movies in theatres nearby and then stroll in to Kwality. This resulted in great popularity and revenue for the newly opened cafe. Another American client, apparently, suggested that Lamba go to the US to see how they made ice cream in factories, Timma narrates. Fearlessly, he undertook that trip in a day and age when air travel was far from common or convenient. And so, the original Kwality ice-cream factory was set up where the restaurant now stands (the brand was sold off to consumer goods company Hindustan Unilever in 1994 and continues to this day as Kwality Walls). Meanwhile, the Americans had also taught Lamba and his partner Iqbal Ghai to make sandwiches, and the duo extended their ice-cream business to a cafe, which sold snacks and coffee too, aside from ice cream.

After Independence, as Punjabi migrants started pouring into Delhi and tastes changed, Punjabi dishes were put on the menu, including the chole bhature that Kwality is now known for (the brand promise is that the bhatura is as big as a football; on most days, it is). P.L. Lamba got the recipe from a Rawalpindi cook while on a trip to Mussoorie, where the cook had settled in the aftermath of Partition. This is the same recipe the restaurant still follows. Chole, or pindi chane as the dish is rightfully called (after Rawalpindi, its place of origin), was not a Delhi dish at all. Chickpeas, as well as that other bean rajma, chicken and paneer travelled from Punjab to Delhi and redefined the capital's restaurant culture.

Today, the butter chicken or chole bhature or saag paneer culture may have waned, and we may be enthralled by our rediscovery of home-style regional cuisines, but Kwality the brand still endures. The refurbished restaurant is still being run with the same passion that its founder had for the business, where he would personally instruct cooks on how to save money on every kilo of potatoes by buying those with fewer 'eyes'! That was the level of personal involvement. Now, his 30-year-old grandson Divij, a Yale graduate, has quit a career in the US to come back home and take over the running of the brand in a similarly hands-on fashion.

As Divij shows me the refurbished premises – a charming balcony that can be turned into a private dining room, a new colonial-looking bar and period memorabilia – and as his mother Timma talks about old recipes that she has retained while making some gravies lighter, it is clear how involved everyone in the family is. This despite the fact that the Lambas are seasoned restaurateurs. They have a thriving catering business and a chain of bakery shops. However, this is a restaurant where the family's roots, history, culture and tastes are closely entwined with the very DNA of the business.

Kwality is not an isolated instance of the owners' 'personalities' having seeped into the business at all levels. Every successful restaurant brand has a personality which comes from its promoter or chef (whoever closely runs it).

The 'vibe' of a restaurant brand is a reflection of its top brass. It is this 'personality' that you can sense as you enter a space, and this is what is served up to you in the product. And a successful brand is one where the personality on the platter finds resonance with its target audience.

The idea of 'soulless' restaurants that many consumers

often talk about is really exactly that – a brand without a distinct, authentic personality, and therefore without any chance at a connect with its audience. Many of you may have come across establishments that you were indifferent to, where you thought the food had 'no soul'. As a restaurant critic and writer, I invariably meet people complaining of this phenomenon.

These restaurants without soul are usually places which are either copycat concepts executed to recreate X restaurant in another city or another part of the world, and/or places in which the owners are not really closely involved. Restaurants like these often fail. Some may make money in the short term, but they can never be successful brands or businesses in the long run.

Real estate czar Harshavardhan Neotia, chairman of the Kolkata-based Ambuja Neotia Group, who also owns some restaurants in eastern India, put it succinctly one day when he was lunching with me at Indian Accent over an extended discussion on the business of restaurants and why people get into it considering it offers such low returns and has such a high failure rate.

'If someone gets into it looking at the money, he will definitely fail. It is important to be genuinely interested in it and be constantly involved, only then can you run a successful restaurant. A small slip, if you are not constantly involved, can cost you the entire business. This is why it is different from other businesses,' he pointed out.

Neotia is right, of course. The restaurant business is highly personal and intensive. You cannot outsource it to consultants if you want to establish a successful brand. Time and again, that approach has failed, and yet so many wannabe restaurateurs flush with funds or having cobbled together 'alliances' of three to four friends, all of whom pool in money and resources, try to set up places where there is no distinct individual vision, where the ideas are borrowed and where the business is remote-controlled. These restaurants are set up only to fail.

Every successful restaurant brand has a certain authentic personality inherent in its DNA, which comes from its owner, creator or chef (if they are involved in the restaurateuring process and not just the kitchen). The personality of a restaurant is not merely about the food it offers, but more about the vibe within, as I have said earlier. That a restaurant has a personality which is a reflection of the restaurateur's does not mean that restaurant brands revolve around individuals, whether chefs or restaurateurs. You don't go to Bukhara, arguably India's most successful restaurant brand, for its chef J.P. Singh. You may not even know that Riyaaz Amlani is the brain behind Social. And while you may have seen pictures of A.D. Singh partying in his restaurants, your decision to go to Olive is unlikely to be affected by that. For the consumer, the restaurant's personality is what matters. This is what they evaluate subliminally, not the individuals. Chef-led restaurants are somewhat different, with chefs themselves becoming celebrities and their personalities then dominating a restaurant's. But in that case, the consumer still comes for a restaurant as a personification of a celebrity.

Often, restaurant experiences are the creation of not one person's thoughts and ideas, but of a small, core team's. In the case of most successful brands, you will find that people in the group are bound by similar values, thoughts and ways of looking at life. That is why they are successful at working together and at making a brand that reflects their common values or vision. You can see examples of this permeating everything in brands like Bukhara and Dum Pukht, two of India's most successful restaurants. Both are owned by ITC Hotels and have been successful for long years because of the sheer depth of research behind them.

Bukhara, such an iconic restaurant, serves relatively simple food – tikkas, dal, tandoori breads. Food similar to what many Indians can easily access at neighbourhood restaurants at a fraction of the price. Why the brand continues to be so successful is because of the far superior quality of the ingredients, the quality of cooking, the consistency of the food produced over the years so that regulars, who form the bulk of the business, who know exactly what they are going for, are never disappointed. But it's also because of the inherent personality of the restaurant and the value system intrinsic to it. While Bukhara's look and feel – its uncomfortable seating, its dining experience where large chunks of food are served and cutlery not provided – is a simulation of hardy and rustic life at a military camp sans refinement, it does not imply a lack of quality in food, service and experience.

It may be trying to lead its diners into an illusion of a rougher life, but as a restaurant experience, it is elevated and very 'luxury'. The value inherent in its DNA is high-end luxury and exclusivity; the high quality of food, formal and attentive service style, top-of-the-line wine and whisky lists, the entire experience all conform to this value.

As a diner, you are always aware that this is a specialized 'experience', created through research into a specific time. Hence you are willing to pay a high price for this exclusivity. This is what I mean by the personality of the restaurant; this sense of inherent exclusivity and all factors coming together to conform to it cannot be copied.

The outer trappings of the 'non-refined' theme have been copied widely, of course, as has been the food – though less successfully, because it is hard to match that quality. However, Bukhara's complete story as a luxury recreation of an army camp and its personality are unmatched, because the attention to detail, the authentic research of its creators and indeed their very own personal sense of luxury as high-quality living cannot be replicated by a copycat. This was part of the group personality of the founders.

Dum Pukht, Bukhara's Awadhi cousin, is its opposite. Instead of the rusticity of the Bukhara experience, here, a courtly culture that produced a highly nuanced cuisine is celebrated. Lucknow is apparent everywhere – not just in the kakori kebabs and dabi dhaki raan, the star dishes, but also in the elaborate courtesy of the service staff, who will tell you '*naush farmaiye*' ('please eat and drink', from a Persian expression that has seeped into Lucknowi Urdu) as they set down the dishes in front of you and exhort you to begin. The Awadhi heritage is apparent in all the stories Ghulam Qureshi, the current chef, tells you about the ingredients and their magical transformation into culinary high art. There are separate water goblets, in different colours, for vegetarians and non-vegetarians, paan and jasmine buds at the end of the meal – all in all, an elaborate immersive experience into a heritage cuisine and culture.

Both Dum Pukht and Bukhara reflect the deep engagement with and research into aspects of Indian history and culture that ITC Hotels has always undertaken. This fits in with the ITC conglomerate's larger brand value of promoting 'Indianness'. In the hotel and restaurant industry, it's commonly said that nobody does Indian better than ITC, and in all my years of writing on restaurants, I find that true.

The hotel chain has restaurant brands of other cuisines, but none of these measure up to the strength of its Indian restaurants. A large part of that credit must go to the personalities, interests, deep knowledge and culture on the part of the top brass, who set standards for food research at ITC Hotels.

I met S.S.H. Rehman one afternoon at his home in Delhi, long after he had retired as the supremo of ITC's food, travel and hotels businesses for many years. (Mr Rehman retired in 2009 after two and a half decades at ITC, though he rejoined the company's board as a non-executive director in 2012.) While I was still a junior writer, Mr Rehman had seemed to follow my work and sent an occasional food book, suitably inscribed, as a gift of encouragement when he particularly liked a piece. I knew him not just by his reputation as a powerful and influential hotelier, but his equally formidable personal reputation of being aristocratic, impeccably well-mannered and charismatic. However, I had never actually met him till I did that afternoon, when I went to his house to chat about the business of building restaurants with the man who had built several legendary ones, including Dum Pukht, Bukhara and Dakshin, three of the most intricately detailed restaurants serving Indian cuisines.

After a brief chat in his study, Rehman invited me to a home-cooked meal. What proceeded defied any ideas of 'home' food in India being necessarily 'homely' or simple. Rehman's trusted cook, under his instructions, had cooked for me a seven-course Hyderabadi meal – various breads, kebabs, gravies, biryani and desserts – each dish presented beautifully as a course. Mr Rehman himself ate little; the entire orchestration was for my benefit. 'Why?' I asked him, completely bowled over by the hospitality, to which he replied, '*Ab aap pehli baar khaane par aayin hai*' ('This is the first time you have come for a meal').

This largesse, this etiquette, is reminiscent of the cultures of Hyderabad and Lucknow, known for their extreme courtesies, graces and *mehmannawazi*, or hospitality. It is this culture that Habib Rehman grew up in, in an aristocratic Hyderabadi family. And though he joined the Indian Army, his lineage is very much a part of his personality. At a restaurant like Dum Pukht, we still see this personality on the platter. Most old hands writing about hotels and restaurants in India know how Mr Rehman shut Mayur, the Indian restaurant at ITC Maurya in Delhi, and opened Bukhara and Dum Pukht in its place, splitting the Indian cuisine of Mayur into two distinct halves – the tandoor based, Punjabi/Frontier, rustic cooking of Bukhara, run by the uber-talented Madan Lal Jaiswal, and the courtly, Awadhi-inspired cuisine at Dum Pukht, which was given to Imtiaz Qureshi to run. Qureshi, a Lucknowi cook, had already been brought in by ITC to run Mayur. With Habib Rehman, who understood that cuisine well, dishes like kakori kebab, raan (originally a tandoor dish, but done in Dum Pukht in a finer fashion) and biryani were tweaked and made appropriate for a more fine-dining experience. How Habib Rehman would sit at long food trials, rejecting or tweaking dish after dish, till the chef was exhausted but the recipe perfected is part of Indian restaurant lore.

Both Bukhara and Dum Pukht have had iconic chefs who helmed the restaurants at their starting in the legendary Madan Lal Jaiswal and Imtiaz Qureshi, whose fame and family have defined the idea of a certain kind of Indian food in restaurants across the globe. Yet the success of the two brands must be credited not just to these iconic chefs. Instead we must see it in the context of the creators of the brands – the team at ITC Hotels led by Mr Rehman, patrons of heritage food who deeply engaged with it. It is their personalities and respect for research that permeates the brands even today.

Over the years, there have been many copies. But since the copycat restaurateurs don't understand the full story or are not rooted in the cultural context, and are not sincere in their research, their 'voice' has never quite rung as true. In a way, this is very similar to an artistic process. For a writer, finding your own distinct voice is vital. It is the same for a restaurant brand. Finding a distinct voice or personality that is a reflection of the restaurateur's own uniqueness is important. Copies do not work, even if well executed, and customers can spot the fakes.

There is a difference between something that naturally flows and something that seems laboured, between a work by Picasso or an imitator. My belief is that the audience can sense this difference subliminally. Just as serious fine-dines need a certain personality to make them successful, I also believe that 'cool' places can only be run by 'cool' people. You have to live a lifestyle to understand it and therefore be capable of building it for your customers.

When the personality of a restaurant/restaurateur is in sync with the aspiration of its target customers, the restaurant works. A Connaught Place eatery in Khan Market or a Khan Market eatery in Connaught Place will not work. This is quite obvious.

But it is astonishing how often potential restaurateurs get this wrong. They fail to analyse either themselves or their market!

Just the other day, as I was walking down Khan Market having finished my writing for the day, I noticed a small dessert parlour. A 10- to 12-seater, it was a new opening, close to L'Opera, the patisserie chain that changed the way Delhi treats fancy sweet nothings. The fledgling bakery store's direct competitors in the same market also include the likes of The Cakery by Big Chill, The Artful Baker, desserts at Café Turtle and Sly Granny, all serving quality desserts.

I walked into the new store and was taken aback. From what I tried, the individually portioned desserts were all stodgy, lacked creativity and looked unappealing. In short, this very obviously looked and tasted amateur. And it was. The cafe is run in collaboration with a pastry school; a young chef is executing the dishes, which may work in a campus store or in a less discerning market than the tony Khan. The store cannot hope to survive in the fiercely competitive area where it has dared to open. Perhaps there is no rent to be paid and perhaps it will be around for a year or two, but I will bet that it cannot hope to create a brand.

As I have said earlier, creating a brand is different from making money. We can see how distinct the two are from the following: At the turn of the millennium, Mumbai was the leading metro when it came to offering consumers unique and quality restaurant experiences. It had quite a few buzzing places if you wanted an interesting evening out. Rain was one of these. A plush restaurant-cum-lounge bar – it was a format that was new to India at that time. It attracted a lot of attention and business. Bollywood stars and their spouses were its regular customers. A flea market every Friday night with fashionable stalls and fortune tellers became the society hangout. The place made a fair bit of money. However, here's the catch: Do you remember it today?

Contrast it to another restaurant-cum-lounge bar that opened the same year. Olive in Mumbai came up in 2000, in a whitewashed bungalow. The site, restaurateur A.D. Singh believes, was inhabited by 'cantankerous spirits'. His wife, Sabina Singh, even got someone to perform an exorcism on the advice of an English clairvoyant and the blue gates were swung open.[2] They remain so till today. It's one of India's iconic brands, with multiple outlets across the country. The vibe that it created two decades ago is still intact today, a number of competitors notwithstanding. It has expanded to Delhi, Bengaluru, Hyderabad and most recently Goa, and is a study in successful brand creation. How has Olive managed to do that? By channelling its restaurateur A.D. Singh's personality. (This is something that we will examine in greater detail in the case studies that follow.)

So we have established that successful brand creators wittingly or unwittingly put bits of themselves into the business. However, this is easier to do with a single restaurant run by the owner or chef. If you are somebody like Chef Bawmra Jap in Goa running a seasonal but highly successful, individualistic restaurant like Bomra's that serves Burmese-meets-Goan at Calangute, you can be content that you have established a successful brand that restaurant-goers from different cities seek out as a destination for dining in itself. However, if your ambition is to expand to a big restaurant company and own multiple outlets of several brands, how does this work? Expansion is a slippery slope indeed, and one that most restaurant companies are grievously sliding down. We'll address that later in the book.

In the rest of this section, we'll look at nine case studies – nine stories – of how India's most successful restaurateurs put their personalities on the platter to create big brands. I will dissect the various approaches each of them has taken to creating these brands and the lessons aspiring restaurateurs can learn from them. The analysis and stories are based on my knowing these restaurateurs for several years and closely interacting with them, often not just professionally, but also as friends.

RESTAURANTS AS STORYTELLING

A.D. Singh, Olive Bar and Kitchen

A.D. SINGH'S PERSONAL STORY seems to be the very embodiment of the lifestyle he offers to his restaurants' customers. You see pictures of him in magazines and the lifestyle pages of newspapers, partying with friends from fashion, the world of arts, films et al. This is exactly the story, the sort of affable glamour that Olive promises you as you walk through its blue doors into its pretty white spaces.

In many ways, AD's best-known brand is an extension of his persona: chic, dapper, casual, urbane. If Olive was a person, it would be AD with his sunny charm. Much of urban, middle-class India aspires to the sophistication that AD possesses and Olive promises.

At the turn of the millennium, the Olive brand helped usher in an era of 'lifestyle' restaurants in India – places admired for their 'vibe', or the stories they communicated through their interiors, service and, of course, food and drink. Once it proved successful, first with the film crowd in Mumbai and then with well-heeled, well-travelled customers in cities like Delhi, there were naturally many competitors and many copycats looking to cash in on its 'Med' theme. In fact, there was a time in the early 2000s when there was a spate of whitewashed restaurants all serving mezzes, pizzas and pastas, all Olive copies. Yet none ever got the personality right: either they were too stiff and trying to impress, or they were downright dowdy. None got the mix of upscale but casual, sophisticated but fun right. No other restaurateur could be an A.D. Singh – a unique personality is a unique personality, after all.

To make matters tougher for copycats, Olive is more than just a pretty place. They could copy its look (if not the vibe) but they could not copy the heart of the brand, which is about solid food and beverage offerings too. Apart from his way of life and personality, AD's uniqueness as a restaurateur has always been his ability to mentor talent and give it a free rein while still being the captain of the ship. He has always had a knack for working together with talented chefs – right from his partnership with Rahul Akerkar (at the beginning of his career) to choosing chefs like Manu Chandra, Dhruv Oberoi and Rishim Sachdeva for Olives in Bengaluru, Delhi and Mumbai.

Whether it is Mumbai or Delhi or Bengaluru or Hyderabad or even Goa (where the food is the least ambitious of all Olives, in keeping with the relaxed, sea-facing vibe), the food at all the Olives is of high quality. The kitchens are helmed by talented chefs, who constantly work towards raising the bar.

Like its managing director, Olive, the brand, is more than a quintessential 'society' face. People come back to it for this inherent quality, not for the prettiness or the company of social A-listers – charms that wear off once the buzz settles.

Interestingly, I have always found AD to be uncomfortable with the tag of 'Page Three restaurateur', something he has been stuck with for almost two decades now. In an interview to me, he once tellingly confessed, 'When people see me at parties, they see me feeding off the energy of people I know, of friends who are happy to see me. But if you put me in a room full of strangers, I may come away without having spoken to anyone. I am a fairly reserved person.'

There is a core of reserve about him and an earnestness that you sense if you know him well. There is substance beyond style as also a quality of always being cognizant of the opinions of others, including those of younger people. Despite being experienced and successful, AD's big plus as a restaurateur is that he is never dismissive of others. This quality has helped him grow the business, as I will explain soon. Before that, let me finish drawing out the parallel between the personality of the restaurateur and his brand.

Olive as a brand clearly shares AD's duality of being serious yet affable. This lightness of being without being a lightweight is critical to the brand's continuing relevance. It makes it attractive to diverse age groups, ensures it doesn't become dated, and also gives it a uniqueness that makes it stand out from the competition. Because of this, Olive is not simply interchangeable with any other social venue.

The intrinsic personality of the brand (serious yet casual, upscale yet not intimidating, with solid food and drink) is found across all Olive outlets. This clarity in conveying to the customer what the brand promise is, and the consistency in dishing it out, is the bedrock on which Olive's (and AD's) credibility and longevity is built. While a focus on quality food as a brand promise may mean lower profits in the short run, to build a long-lasting brand, this credibility is important – not least if you, as a restaurateur, are also going to seek private investment to grow your company. (According to restaurant insiders, when AD and the Olive group sought funding for the first time, they apparently got a higher valuation than the industry standard because of AD's personal credibility.)

As the original Olive patrons in every city have grown older, their children and other younger customers have kept returning to the brand. Thursdays at Olive, its brunches and so on never seem to become passé, unlike many other brands that begin to lose steam after a few years. In Olive's case, a 20-year-old brand has managed to stay relevant to 20-year-olds as well as those in their 40s or 60s. As I mentioned earlier, but must underscore again, it is the brand's unique personality, the mix of an approachable yet stylish vibe, consistent quality and rigorous innovation that keeps it relevant.

AD was born in Delhi but moved to Mumbai (then Bombay) and studied at some of the best institutions there. In the days before foreign education was so widely accessible, he got a scholarship at Lafayette College, Pennsylvania, and gained exposure to the young American life of the grand 1980s, when the US economy was booming and its middle class flush with green. He got back to India and started working in premier companies like TCS and Cadbury's before chucking boring corporate life – to first spend a year with various NGOs and then start his events and party management company, Party Lines, in 1988.

Coming from a privileged, upper-middle-class background with an education and exposure not available to many people in the country at that time, AD was undoubtedly a society front-bencher. Using all these advantages creatively, he started hosting boat parties for the hip crowd in Bombay and soon showed an entrepreneurial streak when he launched Just Desserts in 1990.

With just ₹50,000, he rented after-hours space from an Irani cafe, which shut at 7.30 p.m. each day, and turned it into a restaurant serving coffee and dinner, changing the look of the place in the evenings, rearranging the furniture and so on. It wasn't as if even the desserts were his own cooking – he would source them from Parsi home cooks. It was an ingenious idea of bringing together talented home cooks, a 'cool' arty vibe and the right kind of crowd that would lap up this kind of an experience.

Since then, AD has been in the business of creating various such 'experiences'. He dabbled with the Latin bar Copa Cabana, with small seafood places (Soul Fry, Soul Kadi) and finally launched Olive Bar and Kitchen in Bandra in 2000.

Olive, of course, is not the only brand under the umbrella of his company Olive Bar and Kitchen. Some of the most visible restaurant brands in the country – SodaBottleOpenerWala (the largest brand under the company's umbrella in terms of national presence, it has eight outlets across four cities) Monkey Bar, Toast and Tonic – are all part of the group, 40 per cent stake in which was picked up by Rabobank-sponsored private equity (PE) fund for ₹100 crore in 2017, after Aditya Birla Private Equity made a complete exit. India Agri Business Fund II became a significant investor in Olive by buying a stake from Aditya Birla Private Equity along with a few other selling shareholders.[3]

However, AD as managing director clearly drives the vision of his restaurant company. How has he done what he has done?

At the core of A.D. Singh's 'experience-led' restaurants is the idea of storytelling. This is a critical element in the establishment of any successful brand that restaurateurs often overlook. What is the story? The clearer and simpler it is, and the more in sync with the restaurateur's personality, the easier it is for audiences to connect with it. Much of consumption, after all, is moved by emotions. If you cannot connect with your audience at an emotional level, you cannot establish a long-lasting brand. It is as simple – or tough – as that.

To create a unique, compelling and clear story is difficult. Olive came before experience-led restaurants really took off. It had a less cluttered playing field. However, even a later brand like SodaBottleOpenerWala exemplifies AD's approach to creating a story.

It is not an Irani cafe. People who complain that SBOW is overrated and not 'authentic' are usually those who have frequented Mumbai's iconic eateries and are well acquainted with Irani cafe food as well as traditional Parsi dishes. SBOW is a hybrid product. It takes elements of an Irani cafe and it takes enough of Mumbai's street food staples to make it easy for anyone only broadly seeking 'Bombay'. All these are packaged together in a restaurant with fun interiors, good service and prices, and a lot of easy familiar food (most people would be comfortable with a vada pav) with some lesser-known, more unusual dishes. Most importantly, it is the 'story' of a dying tradition that induces nostalgia.

The entire look and feel of SBOW is a more stylized version of the old Irani cafes. For people who have never been inside one, this is nostalgia packaged with aspiration!

Many people who frequent SBOW and think they are finally eating at an Irani cafe, without being inconvenienced by the shabbiness of history, have obviously bought into this story. The 'berry pulao' for them is aspirational, offering a glimpse into Parsi food, at the same time without being 'too exotic' or too unfamiliar to their palates. They may not have come again and again for an elaborate Parsi meal with more dishes like patra ni machchi (fish coated in a green, coconut masala, wrapped in a banana leaf and steamed), saas ni machchi (a wedding special, fish in a white sauce poured over yellow rice), jardaloo sali boti (meat with apricots), versions of offal or khichri. A few dishes like the berry pulao which are not so challenging to, say, a customer in Delhi, make for easy acceptance. Yet these are also aspirational, with people coming away satisfied at having tried something new. On the other hand, you also have a number of customers who would still surely go for the tried and tested, happy to get vada pav in a quirky, clean, stylish setting. This too is ultimately an aspirational experience.

A wide demographic enjoys the story of the Irani cafe (with

comfortable Mumbai street food) and has bought into it. This is behind the success of SBOW as a brand. Interestingly, the first branch opened in Gurugram's Cyber Hub – a restaurant zone surrounded by large offices, and frequented by corporate executives who may have travelled to Mumbai on work often, and who may have aspired to enjoy its culture (but in a non-challenging way), or were attracted by a certain somewhat sepia-tinted idea of Maximum City. SBOW gave them something new to aspire to while presenting the 'nostalgia' story. It is debatable how the brand would have fared if the first outlet had opened in Mumbai itself, where customers would be more familiar with the fare.

A story that is unique and tugs at a customer's heart while being aspirational is at the core of an experience-led brand's success. Before coming up with a concept, a restaurateur should always ask themselves: What is the story? They should then refine the idea to be clear and consistent in what they are telling the customers (in the case of SBOW, it is simply, 'Irani cafe') and then build in different layers to attract a wider audience (Mumbai street food, activities in the restaurant and so on).

Some stories, however, don't quite click. Lady Baga, another brand by AD's company, has not been successful. Built around the story of a Goan shack, its name a play on Lady Gaga, it sought to attract both an older crowd with nostalgia for a certain kind of Goa of the flower children and a younger crowd for whom Goa is a popular and common party destination.

The first outlet came up in Delhi's Connaught Place in 2016 and another in Mumbai.

AD told me in a conversation for a story I was writing for the *Economic Times* in 2017 that there was a problem with the consistency of food in Delhi with what kind of food did they want to serve (home-style, shack-style or fusion), with the sourcing of ingredients, and also the location in Connaught Place, which as a market seemed to be in a phase where only cheap liquor and North Indian flavours found acceptance.

All these factors may be valid. However, as an analyst, I feel there is a problem with the story of the brand as well. Leaving aside operational problems, and the quality or consistency of the food, the 'Goa shack' story itself may not have the kind of aspiration or nostalgia that AD may have been hoping for with large chunks of consumers.

Many people in India now travel quite frequently to Goa, and more have been more exposed to shacks there than to Irani restaurants, which are a dying genre. Both shack food and other Goan cuisines like its Saraswat and Catholic cooking are enjoying a resurgence and millennials who aspire to lost regional foods have already been going to Goa and discovering family-run places serving these. Lady Baga doesn't fit that bill. It is a recreated shack/Goan-themed place without the charm of the sea; millennials would much rather travel twice or thrice a year to the state and have their fill.

You may ask why some other Goan restaurants outside the state, primarily in Mumbai, have then succeeded? My analysis is this: Many of these are family-run places with a different ethos and different customers. They are not about the 'experience' but mainly about homely cooking. Their audience comes in for the quality of the cooking. Also, in Mumbai these restaurants have an audience already familiar with coastal flavours, with Goans staying in the city, and with a niche foodie audience. Moreover, they are niche restaurants not necessarily known to a much larger pool of people outside their limited geographical area.

Then there is a brand like O Pedro in Mumbai that came up in 2017, which is also a recreation of Goan food, and has managed to establish itself as a top restaurant in Mumbai. It is still too early to say how long it will last, but its success and popularity, to my mind, can be attributed to a few key factors, which are very different from Lady Baga. O Pedro is a chef-led restaurant, where both Floyd Cardoz, who is Goan and has created many of the dishes, and Hussain Shahzad, who is very talented and has spent time in Goa to learn the nuances of the cuisine, keep working on dishes, recreating their versions of classics and tweaking offerings in response to customer feedback.

Then, of course, it is also playing in an area and a subculture that the O Pedro restaurateurs understand: millennial, suburban Mumbai, where the residents are mostly professionals and exposed through travel to various countries, cuisines and cultures. This audience is receptive to their offering, which includes a bar with snazzily presented small bites. If O Pedro decided to grow into a chain, it may not work, because to find a wider audience similarly receptive to these flavours and presentations would be tough in cities and subcultures that the owners and their personalities are not in sync with.

Lady Baga may have worked with a sharper focus on what kind of cuisine and Goa story it was selling, with better quality and consistency of cooking and definitely as a single outlet in a market understood by the Olive team and in sync with the product, rather than as a chain.

In fact, a very important factor in building a strong restaurant brand – and one that AD usually excels at – is the idea of 'personalized' restaurants. In our many conversations over the years, it has become apparent how strongly A.D. Singh believes in the idea that, at its core, a 'lifestyle' restaurant is about offering customers a feeling of connecting with individuals. Usually the chef, and sometimes the restaurateur. If Olive is AD, other brands have other people who are the 'faces', who can be built up like brands themselves, and who can find a personal following that hopefully translates into more business but certainly a stronger brand presence. This marketing tool is employed very well in the instance of SBOW and Toast and Tonic which have talented chefs like Anahita Dhondy and Manu Chandra representing their brands effectively in the media and on social media.

Chains with multiple outlets can become boring assembly-line productions, but the moment a brand has a face, even if these are chains and depend on their larger staff – as much on good line cooks as on their executive chefs – they become more relatable. Every experience-led restaurant attempts to thus establish its chef as a brand. This is a tough balancing act for a restaurateur – and one which we will delve into in another chapter. If they have the interpersonal skills to pull it off, as AD seems to, the marketing strategy can reap rich dividends.

One of A.D. Singh's biggest failures was Ai, a sprawling 12,000 sq. ft restaurant launched in a mall in Delhi's Saket area in 2008. Ai came up as the first standalone Japanese restaurant in Delhi, helmed by Sabyasachi Gorai, who travelled to Japan and researched the cuisine. This was a time when only expensive hotel restaurants like Wasabi offered sushi and sashimi. Ai could have been a trendsetter – and it did usher in the idea of pot-stickers and nigiri rolls in standalones – but it was a financial disaster. Done at a humongous cost, it was a lesson to Singh that times had changed, people wanted smaller, more casual, more cost-effective spaces (while still wanting an 'experience'), and that restaurants had to be lean to make money.

Instead of shutting it down, AD continued to run it – a lesson against emotional attachment, which seems inevitable in passion projects, but which prudent restaurateurs must guard against. Eventually, though, he had to give up; four and a half years later, in 2013, it was reincarnated as Guppy by Ai in a 2,200 sq. ft space at 20 per cent of the cost of the original. It continues to do well in Delhi. The right story at the right price is tough to cook!

WEST DELHI BOY, SOUTH BOMBAY GIRL

Vikrant Batra, Cafe Delhi Heights, and
Gauri Devidayal, The Table

AS I SIT IN Vikrant Batra's West Delhi home one afternoon, eating a meal cooked by his mother – there is her special 'butter chicken' on the menu, tart with the freshness of tomatoes and not sweetened, unlike at many restaurants – I finally understand what lies at the heart of Cafe Delhi Heights and its success as the quintessential Delhi brand.

Throughout the piping hot meal, as I am urged to eat 'one more' phulka and Mrs Usha Batra urges me to think of her as my own mother, there is no getting away from the large-hearted Punjabi culture of the household: generous hospitality, overflowing gregariousness and a knack for making of the other your own.

This is what led to the flourishing of Punjabi enterprise in Delhi following Partition and this is what infuses much of the city's spirit today. The quieter reserve that we find in many other subcultures is absent in West Delhi's Punjabi homes.

As we continue, Vikrant also promises me an autograph

of 'Virat', the Indian cricket captain Virat Kohli, who grew up in the same neighbourhood and whose older brother is friends with Vikrant. Both Kohli and Vikrant are part of the West Delhi subculture, where emotion and personal bonds are often on display, but also ambition and a competitive drive.

In the mid-1970s, Vikrant's father walked out of his joint family business. To make ends meet, Vikrant told me, his enterprising mother set up an embroidery unit and ran a garments business from the family's small house. Eventually, the unit made export-quality garments for brands like GAP and the family was able to expand the site that was both their business and home. Then, business began to go down. Mrs Batra decided to take up fabricating for tent houses, and soon after, when she saw that banqueting was a good business, the hardy Punjabi matriarch showed great acumen and started Batra Banqueting in 1989.

All the workers from the stitching and embroidery unit were now turned into cooks! The family started a banquet hall in the area, with Mrs Batra manning it. Vikrant was studying in Class 9 at the time. His mother would ride a scooter, shop for vegetables, cook tiffins and pick him up from school. After school, he would help in the kitchen and get free spring rolls and chilli chicken as payment. There was very little outside exposure, but Vikrant and his older brother Sharad (both now partners in their restaurant company) helped their mother, managing the banquet hall while still in school and college.

After he graduated with a degree in commerce from Hindu College, Vikrant Batra wanted to expand the food business. More floors were added to the banqueting hall, more caterings undertaken, and finally, in 1996, Sharad, who had started dabbling in real estate, bought a property in Gurugram (then Gurgaon) and took up a Nirula's franchise. Vikrant joined him, studying at Fore School of Management in the evenings, running the Nirula's outlet during the day, as well as a thriving West Delhi catering company.

There was money but the hours were thankless. In 2008, Vikrant did his last wedding catering job, and took a year off to think about what he wanted to do. The next year, he opened his first Café Delhi Heights in Rajouri Garden, a moneyed West Delhi enclave. He wanted to run it on a Barbecue Nation format, offering his customers unlimited buffet meals for a set price. The restaurant was called a cafe because Batra had been impressed, he told me, with his maiden visit to Pali Village Cafe in Mumbai.

Now came the crucial phase of the quintessentially West Delhi entrepreneurs getting out of their cultural comfort zone and going to glitzy Gurugram. In 2011, because Sharad had acquired a property at a mall in Gurugram, they opened a second Café Delhi Heights outlet there. But this time, Vikrant decided to do it in a completely different format.

Instead of all-you-can-eat buffets catering to a market that prized quantity, the emphasis shifted to 'inventiveness' and quirky plating to appeal to a slightly more sophisticated audience, one that was aspirational and millennial, instead of the family groups who frequented the original restaurant. This was the time that 'modern Indian' cuisine – familiar flavours served in inventive presentations – was at its peak, and casual restaurants sought to emulate what had already been done at Indian Accent or Masala Library.

The Batras however, always conscious of price, were also going to play the 'value' game they knew well from their West Delhi businesses. The new restaurant in Gurugram bled for 18 months. In the meantime, having sought another property in the city's Ambience Mall, the Batra brothers decided to risk opening another outlet. Finally, the tide turned.

As food groups and social media posts gained ground, Cafe Delhi Heights' Juicy Lucy burger and assortment of comfort dishes, which really were not anything new but sold in quirky presentations at competitive prices, became well known. The restaurant became a brand. West Delhi's tastes and sensibilities – a certain warmth built into the experience, big-hearted portions, price cuts, bold, familiar flavours – all coalesced to make a brand that would appeal to a millennial audience that shared these sensibilities and tastes, even if this was south of South Delhi, not in Rajouri Garden.

What the Batras knew best – familiar, Punjabi-led bold flavours done at lower prices but packaged smartly – both in their banqueting business and early trysts with restaurateuring is still what they do best.

Cafe Delhi Heights represents a certain Delhi and therefore works quite well in several pockets in the metropolis. I am sure it can also work quite well in many other markets/cities that are dominated by students and young executives because of a certain globalization of taste and lifestyle and shared pop culture. But even so, because it reflects a specific sensibility, it may not have the same resonance away from its home ground of the NCR.

The brand made its Mumbai debut in 2016 in Lower Parel, but it hasn't been able to make the same kind of an impression there. Aamchi Mumbai and saadi Dilli are different personalities, after all.

Now, let us train our lens on The Table in Colaba, South Mumbai. It is one of India's most premium restaurants, built around California-style sensibilities with a focus on fresh, high-quality ingredients. The Table resonates with an international, well-travelled audience very different from the one Cafe Delhi Heights caters to.

Gauri Devidayal, The Table's co-owner, belongs to an old, well-known family in Mumbai. She grew up on Altamont Road and now lives with her husband and business partner Jay Yousuf on Napean Sea Road. A law graduate from University College London and a qualified chartered accountant, Gauri had a comfortable career abroad, where she worked at KPMG and PriceWaterhouseCoopers and lived in London for eight years before moving back to Mumbai. Jay, for his part, stayed for many years in California and was exposed to different cultures and culinary experiences before the two decided to set up their maiden venture in their home ground of South Mumbai. The Table came up in 2011, around the same time that the Batras were setting up Cafe Delhi Heights in its present form in Gurugram.

Gauri's background as a 'South Bombay girl', her upbringing, her stints working internationally, and therefore her sensibilities, lifestyle and personality, could not be more dissimilar to Vikrant Batra's. The restaurants the two set up show these differences quite clearly. Gauri's is a cosmopolitan, elite space (The Table is categorized as a casual fine-dine by its restaurateurs) which works on the premise of quality but also exclusivity, even if it is casual in its service style. Vikrant's restaurant is for a more mass audience and works on the twin keys of affordability and popular robust flavours that appeal to a broader base of consumers.

The question to ask ourselves as analysts is, could these two very different people have come up with successful restaurants completely at variance from their own personalities? What if Gauri Devidayal attempted a Cafe Delhi Heights? And Vikrant Batra attempted something like The Table? Could they pull these off?

The answer must be a firm no – at least to my mind. Gauri has stayed firmly within her own broad social milieu with The Table and other ventures like Magazine Street Kitchen (a collaborative space where visiting chefs host dinners with tasting menus) and Miss T (a bar). All her restaurants cater to a pool of diners who very possibly have similar sensibilities to those of her social set. Vikrant does that with Cafe Delhi Heights, where the subculture of the audience is familiar to him from his own life experience.

He, however, did attempt a restaurant, if not similar to The Table, then something in the same genre: Nueva, a 'South American' restaurant and bar. In opening this, Vikrant stepped out of his comfort zone, I feel, which is his affinity with the mass, young 'Delhi' culture. He has no connection to South America that we know of and the kind of audience that he has been used to serving at Cafe Delhi Heights would presumably not have any affinity or exposure to South American culture or cuisine either. Most of this audience would also not be cosmopolitan or multicultural enough to identify with a lesser-known global cuisine/bar culture. It is inexplicable to me why Vikrant chose to go in for this format. Despite many marketing efforts and events that I still see around it, it does not seem to have enough brand recall, to my mind.

Restaurants reflect the personalities of people who own or run them. They are businesses that are a product of a certain culture and milieu, reflect certain lifestyles and, at their most successful, cater to people who share the same cultural values or environment. In this they are unlike many other businesses, wherein people are less important than processes.

Rapid Fire

- **What makes a restaurant successful?**

  Batra: Food.

  Devidayal: A great quality product in terms of food and beverage, warm accommodating hospitality and a great vibe. Over time, consistency and uncompromising quality.

- **What is the most common mistake a new restaurateur makes?**

  Batra: Uncontrolled expense. If you go wrong in the beginning only with rent or spend too much money on interiors right at the start without realizing what your return on investment is, you cannot make it right ever.

  Devidayal: Cutting costs on things which one should never compromise on. Doing a concept because it worked for someone else rather than because it is something one truly believes in.

- **How much should your investment be?**

  Batra: For a 1,500–3,000 sq. ft place, ₹2–3 crore. Rent must not cross 10–12 per cent. If you can do this, profit could be 15–20 per cent [in formats such as Batra's].

  Devidayal: Depends on the kind of restaurant, whether licences are in place or not (it's a huge expense). Generally, one should budget ₹15,000 per sq. ft, factoring a buffer for delays, losses, working capital. [In a luxury, fine-dine format such as what she owns, the EBITDA margin is 15 per cent.]

- **Most important support?**

  Batra: Vendor support is important. For 27 years, we have the same vendors and payment is always sorted. We have an inventory of ₹1.5 crore in a store of 7,500 sq. ft. My mother looks after it.

Devidayal: Key people are a reliable bar manager, general manager and executive chef, who understand and have the same values of quality and hospitality. A good person doing PR and marketing is also important. As the business grows, a good HR manager and accountant are important.

INDIA'S MOST WANTED

Riyaaz Amlani, Impresario

IT IS JUST ANOTHER day in Mumbai – impossibly humid, unimaginably chaotic. But in Riyaaz Amlani's spacious Bandra apartment with an enviable view of the sea, all of the city's discomforts lie forgotten. We experience a moment of joie de vivre being in this always-on-the-move city sometimes brings.

A birthday has been celebrated, Riyaaz's toddler son Khayal has been sitting on the table waiting for a piece of the cake, the balcony curtains are billowing in the sea air, Riyaaz is trying to order a snack for his wife Kiran from his phone app even as he says bye to his visiting mother, who is going back to her home in another part of the city, and at the same time trying to settle me into his study, so that we can begin the tête-à-tête for a piece I would eventually write.

'Are you comfortable?' he asks, a question that comes up repeatedly throughout our conversation. 'Would you like coffee?' his mother asks one last time before she leaves. I decline. 'Riyaaz will make it for you, if you want it later,' she tells me as we bid each other goodbye.

Great, so this is a gender-equal household, I mentally note, feeling happy at the small detail that I have observed. It is contrary to this mental image I (and perhaps others) have of Riyaaz heading a sort of a big boys' club within the Indian restaurant industry, where restaurateurs both established and aspiring often call him 'Riyaaz bhai'.

Though he is no longer the president of the National Restaurant Association of India, an industry group with nationwide membership, Riyaaz is widely recognized within the food industry as having united what was a motley bunch of fewer restaurateurs into a powerful lobbying group – an entity that tries to influence both policymakers and customers through various outreach tools.

Restaurateurs I have met and spoken to have always had a good word about Riyaaz and his extreme responsiveness to any of their problems – anything from multiple, confusing laws governing the business to harassment while getting the many licences and permits needed to open a restaurant in India.

An alpha personality with the ability to bring together many different people into a collective through some sort of an unspoken code, wherein the group stands for all and all stand for the group, is perhaps responsible for Riyaaz's success.

These same qualities were evident, if a little more subdued, in his early years as a restaurateur too, when his image as a biker boy leading a close-knit bunch of friends with similar interests coincided with his image as a restaurateur.

Social, one of the most successful casual dining brands in the country, changed all that. But we are getting ahead of our story.

Any successful leader, whether of a business, an industry or a biker's group, must by definition be available to others and be solicitous of their interests even as he/she goes about looking after his/her own. The leader must make his/her followers believe that he/she will stand by them through thick and thin.

This ability to inspire confidence and be there for his people is what defines Riyaaz, in my opinion. It is evident in how solicitous he is of me and my comfort through a very long interview. And it is evident in his restaurants as well.

One minor point he mentions in passing while I prod him on this and that about his business is that he wants customers in his restaurants to 'be comfortable'. This really is key to how he functions as a restaurateur when he creates a brand. And this is, I believe, critical to the overwhelming popularity of his restaurants with their millennial customers.

As a student in Los Angeles, Riyaaz was on a shoestring budget with money to fund his studies only for one semester. He lived far away from the campus and could not socialize much with his peers because, as he told me, the last train left at 9 p.m. and he had to be on it to get back home. One evening, he recalled, back in his residential neighbourhood, sad and lonely, he went to a cafe owned by somebody called Victor. 'I didn't know anyone and must have been sitting sadly. Victor saw me and started introducing me to everyone. I finally found a sense of belonging in that cafe,' he said.

This experience, he told me during that interview, was his biggest influence as a restaurateur. In fact, we can see this concept of restaurants as primarily social spaces in his various brands. When he launched Mocha in 2001 with two other friends (each invested ₹5 lakh in the business, and Impresario, the parent company, was born), the idea was to create a comfortable 'coffee with conversation' space for the young Gen Y. In 2014, when Social launched in Hauz Khas Village in Delhi, the idea was still the same – a space where millennials could just be themselves, a space that could be their workspace or living room or bar or dining room and where they could bond with others who shared their subculture and lifestyle.

Riyaaz has always been at his best and most successful creating restaurant spaces where different people feel they can find a sense of belonging. Victor's cafe may have been a one-off. But Riyaaz has converted that into a larger theme for his business across brands. His customers connect with the restaurant and the community it fosters and all become part of a larger cultural community.

With 23 outlets in cities including Mumbai, Delhi, Bengaluru and Pune (at the time of writing), it is a hugely successful restaurant format, but Social has been a social experiment too. It ushered in the breakthrough idea in metropolitan India of shared spaces for the young that could transform into co-working spaces, all-day cafes, high-energy bars, and performance and event venues instead of being merely dining and drinking spaces.

We are now in the thick of the gig economy. Consumers no longer frequent restaurants – or at least certain kinds of restaurants – only on special occasions. Instead, restaurants are part of an urban lifestyle in which places of work are no longer fixed, populations are floating and disparate people are now connected through social media and share a fairly similar culture if they belong to roughly the same age and income groups. In this more informal, more collaborative world, codes of behaviour too have altered. A drink is no longer a decadent indulgence or something at the beginning of a binge. You could order one while working on your laptop out of a cafe and certainly while conducting a business meeting.

Riyaaz was among the first lot of entrepreneurs in India to realize this shift in urban lifestyle, and also one of the first to build his products to cater to this huge change that has come about only in the past five to six years. As a place which can be something for everyone, Social has a huge resonance with its audience and copycats have not dented its following.

I was a regular customer at the co-working space when it first launched in Hauz Khas Village. In fact, I wrote a major part of my first book, *Mrs LC's Table*, from Social, a space where in those early months of 2014–15 I met so many interesting entrepreneurs and start-up kids, all of whom had made it into a sort of cool office space. We would chat while taking breaks, sometime eat our lunches together, and in general have a good time, bonding while working.

Most of us who were regulars then also felt a bond with the staff manning the space. The young culture managers, always up to new, cool stuff (I was once featured in an in-house video they made on Social regulars, circulated just to the community of users of the space, as having the most interesting job in the country), and even to the service staff, occasionally ready to give you a free coffee if you walked in really early in the morning, as a gift for a cheery day ahead.

It is obvious from the success of the brand that many more people across India have connected with it. But this connection, so crucial to the brand's success and so hard to replicate, comes from Riyaaz's personality, which in turn has been shaped by his own experiences.

By his own confession, he is very interested in pop culture and clued into it. 'I have a fear of missing out on cultural trends, and hang out with many young people,' he told me at one point in our conversation. Social is also a cultural space, connecting with audiences through music, films and performances, which change as the brand goes from city to city. The design reflects the cultural sensibilities of every market and gets tweaked in each outlet as newer ones are added to keep pace with changing time and geography.

On the other hand, I never really cared about the food or drink at any of the Socials. While much was made of on social media about its Long Island iced tea when the brand launched and the quirky crockery (which seemed to me fit for a hospital), these gimmicks are not why Social's customers go back to it. These fads may have made an outlet buzz initially, but at the core of the brand is a larger cultural sensibility and a desire to let a customer be 'comfortable' in their own skin. Any brand that tries to emulate Social by copying only the superficial gimmicky ideas cannot hope to succeed – because at its heart is a much deeper sensibility that is hard to replicate.

It is interesting to hear Riyaaz confess that he is not really 'fond' of food. It is my opinion that his most successful brands are not led by food, because what makes him as a person tick is his ability to bring people together via pop culture and design. The core of a restaurateur's personality inevitably defines his restaurants and draws an audience in sync with it.

Which is why I find Riyaaz's latest business strategy interesting. He knows that he is good at design and in establishing what he calls the 'tonality' of a restaurant. He also believes that a large restaurant company can only focus on just two or three brands with a big footprint if it is to sustain them. But to be able to open and sustain more successful brands (which need to be individualistic and intimate and therefore connect with audiences), a big company must operate like a mom-and-pop one.

After the mega buyout of a controlling stake in Impresario

by the private equity fund L Catterton Asia, the investment arm of French luxury conglomerate LVMH, the smartest move he has made is investing in partners who are chefs/food creators strong on a particular food concept and want to open their own restaurants without necessarily having to go through birthing pains. (Riyaaz retains a 20–25 per cent stake in the business and continues to be the CEO, according to a report after the buyout in the *Economic Times* in 2017.) He seeks out these small, individualistic restaurateurs and chefs and helps incubate their brands under his company's umbrella. Slink and Bardot, a small bar with French food and a French chef and restaurant manager who are partners in the business, is a step in that direction. Earlier in 2019, Riyaaz teamed up with Prashant Issar and Anuj Shah, who earlier ran a restaurant called Mirchi and Mime that employed hearing- and speech-impaired service staff. This concept has now been transplanted at Ishaara in partnership with Riyaaz, where despite the concept being unique in India, it is still the food that is likely to draw customers back. Issar had worked as chef under Camellia Panjabi in London and that pedigree shows in the solid classical underpinnings of every dish, despite some modern presentations.

Riyaaz told me of his vision to invest in various small brands managed by different partners when I had profiled him in 2017, and this is now all too apparent. This is one way to grow viably. Once again, this business strategy too hinges on his ability to bring people of different talents and abilities together.

Needy restaurants fail

In 2011, Riyaaz Amlani built a restaurant for himself, as he'll tell you. Smoke House Room in Crescent Mall, Delhi, was an ambitious place, with fine dining, fine crockery, a fine view of the Qutab Minar and so on. 'It was me trying to show everything I had learnt. It was a cathedral to my ego,' he said. It was a needy restaurant that demanded reverence for its food and for the pricey experience it was supposedly offering its customers. It did not fly.

Riyaaz says he lost ₹12 crore in the process – ₹7 crore to build the restaurant, ₹5 crore to keep it afloat (he kept it on for two years because he could not bear to shut it down). Meanwhile, he was losing money elsewhere too. Mocha was hit by the hookah ban that the state of Maharashtra imposed in 2011. Because of the after-effects of the 2008 economic downturn, his investors in other projects had also backed out by then, but he could not get out of these and had to keep going. Out of this debris appeared Social.

Riyaaz today believes that 'needy' restaurants do not work. Very few chefs (and very few experiences) can command a kind of reverence from the audience. When he opened Social, it was with the thought of doing the exact opposite of what he had done with Smoke House Room. Instead of the niche audience for the fine-dine, the thought was to find the widest base possible with a mass product. Instead of fine, cheffy food, the idea was how to sell anda bhurji; instead of choosing expensive crockery and cutlery with care, here was mismatched, cheap stuff, and even the plaster on the walls was stripped off to give it a grunge look.

Social was a reaction to failure. It became Riyaaz Amlani's biggest success. Perhaps he was at the right place and the right time with a product that was needed by the gig economy. Or perhaps, he had returned to his own personal comfort zone of creating spaces where people would feel 'comfortable' vis-à-vis a restaurant that would intimidate and demand attention for itself. What is certain is that the brand and the personality were in sync and they clicked.

THE INVISIBLE RESTAURATEURS

Rohit Khattar, Old World Hospitality, and
Sameer Seth, Hunger Inc.

ROHIT KHATTAR, WHO OWNS Indian Accent, India's most celebrated Indian restaurant, and the only one from the country on the coveted Asia's 50 Best Restaurants list, and Sameer Seth, who co-owns The Bombay Canteen, the famous Mumbai restaurant, have widely different experience levels in the world of restaurants. Khattar, a veteran in the world of restaurateuring, has seen the ups and downs of the industry from the 1990s onwards, when Seth was still in school, and as such it is impossible to compare their careers.

Their best-known restaurants are completely different entities too – The Bombay Canteen is casual and in an entirely different category from the luxury-dining, stylized experience at Indian Accent. However, as a personality and entrepreneur, I find Seth to be naturally like Khattar.

This comparison is going to surprise many, including the two protagonists themselves. But having known them for a while, it's clear to me that their shared traits of being measured, methodical and reluctant to step into any kind of limelight have helped them build successful restaurants and navigate the tricky tightrope of captaining their ships while working with celebrity chefs who are intrinsic to their restaurant brands, and who are in fact brands in themselves.

Claus Meyer, the legendary restaurateur and co-founder of Noma, has often been credited as the father of modern Nordic gastronomy. Meyer opened Noma in Copenhagen in 2003, a restaurant based on his idea of cooking only with local Scandinavian ingredients. Before the restaurant, which would go on to find phenomenal global following, Meyer hosted a TV show on Danish national television called Meyer's Kitchen, in which he expounded his philosophy of food based on a rediscovery of local ingredients, flavours and ways of cooking or preserving food. The show ran from 1991 to 1999, helping increase awareness about local restaurants in Scandinavia, which helped them develop their own idiom instead of French and Italian cooking. During this time, Meyer also got 10 of the region's top chefs to sign a manifesto devoted to bringing lost regional flavours into restaurants and presented this manifesto to journalists, after which the movement rapidly spread not just all over Scandinavia, but across the globe.

In 2003, Meyer opened Noma, hiring a 25-year-old, unknown chef named Rene Redzepi to head its kitchen.

Within two years, Redzepi had won his first Michelin star and would go on to make Noma one of the top restaurants in the world. In the process, the chef amassed a huge following himself and became a global celebrity – even though within Scandinavia and within international restaurateuring circles, Meyer too needs no introduction. The two men responsible for turning Copenhagen into a global dining destination, however, became estranged, according to industry buzz, cited by the *Guardian* in a 2016 article.[4]

Redzepi had also mentioned to the *Wall Street Journal* in 2013[5] that he had become so frustrated that he gave Meyer an ultimatum: 'It's you or me, Claus.' That discussion ended with Meyer selling a chunk of his majority stake in Noma to another investor while Redzepi became the main owner.

On a cold winter evening in Delhi, I met Meyer at the Danish embassy at a reception hosted in his honour and asked him the one important question no one else seemed to have broached: the biggest challenge of being a restaurateur. To my surprise and journalistic delight, the candid restaurateur replied, 'Managing the delicate relationship with the chef.'

In today's times, when social media and traditional media have made chefs into stars, whose front-of-the-house visibility is important, and Instagram following contributes to a restaurant's success, it is important to build the chef as a brand. Meyer pointed this out rightly during our conversation, but to manage the chef after he becomes a star – 'especially if he is a complex person', as Meyer said to me – is tough for any restaurateur, who must necessarily be dependent on their star chef and yet also be the captain of the business.

When I see Khattar and Seth, I admire how adroitly the two have been able to navigate their interpersonal and professional relationship with the two chefs who are the faces of their respective restaurants. Manish Mehrotra and Thomas Zacharias are brands with huge followings, and Zacharias is now a partner in The Bombay Canteen as well. But Khattar and Seth as primary investors run the businesses closely. They have been able to maintain the fine balance of letting their chefs grow while remaining in control because of their intrinsic personalities, of which a key trait is the love for invisibility.

They are happy to let others bask in the glow of fame – while they work their restaurants with a sharp-eyed meticulousness that is rare in the Indian restaurant-scape.

Rohit Khattar is arguably the most successful restaurateur in the country, and it is not just because he has created and owns Indian Accent. He is perhaps the only restaurateur with an almost 100 per cent record of success. Virtually every restaurant he has opened in the past 25 years has been a success. Whether it is Chor Bizarre (serving pan-Indian food), or the restaurants at the India Habitat Centre, Oriental Octopus (one of my favourite restaurants in Delhi, and the place where Manish Mehrotra started out) or lately Comorin, a mixed-format restaurant with a sophisticated bar and Manish Mehrotra's small plates, all enjoy popularity, monetary success and brand recall.

For someone of this stature, it is shocking that Rohit has hardly ever bagged any 'restaurateur of the year' awards at the two score or more food awards in the country. Even more surprisingly, he is rarely written about. One of the few articles ever done on him was one I had written for the *Economic Times*. Rohit spent half of that interview – over a lunch comprising of the two things that are apparently his favourite foods, tabak maaz and chaat – trying to convince me not to write the piece! In fact, this elusiveness has been inherited by his son Rishiv, who ideated on and launched Comorin in Gurugram in late 2018, but steadfastly refuses to be featured anywhere.

At first, I used to think that Rohit Khattar's apparent reluctance to be in the limelight was simply an image of reticence. Indeed, there are people who may seek such an image of exclusivity, but with them it is only a facade.

In Rohit's case, however, I soon realized, this is a genuine part of his personality. 'There are restaurateurs who enjoy the limelight and want to be the face of their brand and there are those who want the chef to be,' he told me once, almost philosophically, claiming that when he launched Indian Accent, it was a conscious decision to put Manish Mehrotra front and centre. The third pillar of his company, the exceptional Old World Hospitality, is Sandeep Tandon, who has been friends with Rohit since school, has a sharp business mind and has been running the company stringently ever since it came up. He is, if possible, even more reticent and meticulous than Rohit.

It's proved to be a happy decision and a happy marriage because it is based on complementary personalities. Manish, ever creative, has no aspiration to become a businessman – he cannot deal with money, the chef says. Rohit, the businessman, enjoys conceptualizing and marketing his brands, but has no aspiration to become the face of the business. Sandeep runs everything keenly. All suit each other. Rohit believes that this is the best possible arrangement. Chefs can of course be restaurateurs too and be both the face and backbone of the business, but it is very hard to do it, especially if you are operating at the highest level in the fine-dining space. 'Chefs like Gordon Ramsay who have spawned an empire have had very steep learning curves. Most have partners who are very solid,' Rohit pointed out.

In tandem with the reluctance to be in the limelight is another character trait: extreme meticulousness and attention to detail. Ask Rohit what makes a restaurant concept successful and he will tell you that it is 'going deep into the concept with regard to food and design and sticking with it'. Consumers may give you feedback and it is important to be cognizant of that, but once the concept has been unrolled (obviously, after great deliberation), the idea must be to stick with it.

It takes an organized and detail-oriented mind to be able to do that. I have witnessed first-hand the kind of detailing that went into the launch of Indian Accent in New York – when professional menu writers were brought in and every word debated to keep the essence of explanations right even while making the Indian dishes comprehensible to an American. And I have also seen the smallest of ways in which Rohit and his wife Rashmi were personally involved with Chor Bizarre when it launched at Bikaner House – the interiors having been furnished with pieces picked out personally by the two and stored in their home before being sent to the restaurant.

Though there is a close-knit core team that has been working with Rohit for years, he and his entire family are deeply involved in the running of his restaurants. At its core, Old World Hospitality is very much a family-owned company, retaining the individualism of its owners even as it runs some of the biggest brands in the country.

The parallel between Khattar and Sameer Seth, whose Hunger Inc. owns The Bombay Canteen, is striking. Like Rohit, Sameer is all about attention to the product rather than attention to himself. Around 2005–07, he had worked for two and a half years with Shalom, a popular Delhi restaurant and lounge bar. At the time, the group that Shalom was the flagship of was rapidly growing and had 11 restaurants under its belt. Sameer as the marketing and finance head was the jack of all trades and oversaw everything, though, he says tongue in cheek, the most important thing to decide at that time about the product was what kind of music would one play!

After the Shalom stint, he went off to study at Cornell University and did a course in restaurant entrepreneurship, during which he spent six months studying and analysing 25 to 30 different restaurants in New York. He wrote a paper on this and then worked in New York as part of the opening team of North End Grill (by Danny Meyer), run by one of the biggest NY restaurant groups, Union Square Hospitality. This is where Sameer met chef Floyd Cardoz, who had earlier headed Danny Meyer's restaurant Tabla. Floyd would mentor Sameer and Yash Bhanage, a fellow student and friend, and the three would team up some years later to open The Bombay Canteen.

In New York, Sameer's biggest learning, he told me, was the attention given to the product and to training the staff. In India, a regular line-up before service, he pointed out, would usually be about things like 'Is your hair cut, nails trimmed or lighter working?' There, at least 30 minutes every day were spent on tasting food and wine in order to understand the menu.

Sameer knew that he wanted to do something with restaurants because he liked interacting with people and liked food – without wanting to be a chef or hogging the limelight himself. And so, the natural step was to open a restaurant. But the meticulous research involved in setting up TBC, not to mention its sister restaurant O Pedro, is unusual in India, where concepts and menus are often prepared by using Google! Before the launch of both the restaurants, key team members travelled to relevant cities (in the case of O Pedro, the Goan restaurant, to Portugal as well) to eat and research. The restaurants are run closely by Sameer and Yash, who are often to be found on the floor themselves. One week before every new menu, even if for a promotion, is rolled out, there are staff tastings and trainings to allow them to know the menu and be able to have conversations with people on new dishes. Everything is strategized, everything is based on data and decisions using that collected data. Nothing is laissez faire.

In fact, I have always been struck by how both Khattar and Seth always seem to think out everything in detail. They are the two toughest restaurateurs to interview because you will almost certainly not catch them off guard This sense of being measured is vital to running restaurants with precision and deliberation rather than in ad hoc, personally whimsical ways, as many owners tend to – an important trait to cultivate for any aspiring restaurateur.

INVENTION IS TRADITION, TRADITION IS INVENTIVE

The MTR Family

TRADITION AND INNOVATION ARE not mutually exclusive. In fact, if a study of various culinary cultures teaches us one thing it is that 'authenticity' is a debatable concept, since cooks the world over have always experimented with ingredients, flavours and cooking styles, influenced by trade, geography, politics, social trends and so on.

In India, restaurateurs who think of setting up 'traditional' or 'soulful' restaurants, as we often think of them, contrasting them with 'modern restaurants' that tend to focus on presentation instead of the kind of complex flavours most Indians are accustomed to, must remember this truth. The Indian customer is, and always has been, used to inventiveness, especially when they are eating out – the restaurant is expected to serve something new or 'different' from what the customer eats at home or during their daily routine.

The irony is that Indian customers are often thought of as conservative – unwilling to try newer foods. Observers of the restaurant business often point out how Indian, Indian-Chinese and Indianized pizza and pasta are the bestselling cuisines in this country, and that there is low acceptance for foreign cuisines. While all this is true, what people don't realize is this: the demanding Indian customer wants both familiarity and novelty at the same time. Restaurants that we now think of as 'traditional', in fact, are often brands built on the bedrock of inventiveness. Nothing exemplifies this inherent contradiction (that still holds true) within the Indian restaurant-scape than a super brand like Mavalli Tiffin Room (MTR) in Bengaluru, one of India's oldest and most celebrated restaurant brands.

In 1920, three brothers, Parameshwara Maiya, Ganappayya Maiya and Yagnanarayana Maiya, from a small village called Parampalli in Karnataka's South Canara district, left home to escape poverty and came to Bengaluru, then Bangalore. The brahmin boys, like many others of their caste, could cook. Parameshwara found employment in an affluent Indian judge's home as a cook. The employer must have taken a shine to him because he assisted the young man and his brother Ganappayya in setting up a tiny eatery selling coffee and 'tiffin' items on the posh Lalbagh Fort Road. Brahmin's Coffee Club opened in 1924 and started growing in reputation.

When Parameshwara died five years after setting up the business, the youngest brother, Yagnanarayana, took over the reins. He proved to be a savvy restaurateur, building the business and the brand, and the eatery grew so popular that affluent Indians started patronizing it too, stopping by for 'car service' – to pick up food in their cars or send their chauffeurs over for it.

By the time the country gained independence, the client base had expanded and its stature had grown even more. In the 1950s, a quarter-century after the coffee club had been first set up, Yagnanarayana, by now firmly driving the business, started thinking of making it bigger. The brothers bought a piece of land near the original eatery and started building a restaurant. Their thoughts now turned to branding, and so in 1960, Mavalli Tiffin Room, named after the locality where it was situated, opened and stands to this day at Lalbagh Road.

If you have ever queued up for breakfast at its doors in the early morning, you would not need me to tell you how popular MTR remains. On weekdays, the Lalbagh Road restaurant caters to about 1,000 to 1,500 people, Hemamalini Maiya, its third-generation co-owner, told me when I met her one day over filter coffee in one of the hidden rooms inside MTR that sometimes functions as her office. On weekends, this number doubles, she adds. Every day, approximately 20 kg of bisibele bath is cooked and sold; 600 to700 idlis are made fresh every morning and by 9 a.m. they are all over, as is the sambar made in huge steel vats, steaming and aromatic with freshly ground spices. MTR is an institution for a reason.

Hemamalini runs the original restaurant and its sister outlets (there are 10 MTRs in India and four abroad at the time of writing) along with her brothers Vikram and Arvind. We sat and sipped filter coffee, a speciality of the restaurant, whose aroma comes from a trademark blend of Arabica and chicory. Over this, I listened to the story of an enterprising family.

As we went through the key moments of their restaurateuring journey, it became evident that MTR the brand owes much of its success to the personality of the youngest of the Maiya brothers, Yagnanarayana, who in fact spearheaded the restaurant's growth after he joined the business. Yagnanarayana, it seems, was always inventing, always full of new ideas, always up for new lessons. In 1951, he decided to undertake a trip to England to see how restaurants functioned there. He came back impressed with the standards of hygiene and cleanliness and soon incorporated steam sterilization of the utensils, crockery and cutlery at his restaurant. MTR still maintains this system; one of the pop legends about the brand is how people would be invited to walk in through its kitchens to see for themselves the level of hygiene. Cleanliness thus became a brand value for MTR, one on which the audience's trust still rests.

On his English sojourn, Yagnanarayana also saw cups and saucers used to serve coffee. Once he returned to Bangalore, he decided to use china in his restaurant too. Coffee began to be poured out of kettles in the family section – instead of sticking with the tumblers used traditionally. Then there were moves like introducing small booklets for customers, giving them instructions on dining etiquette. Hema and I laugh as we go over the list of dos and don'ts. People were told not to comb their hair in the dining hall, to keep the curry leaves in their plates and not on the tables, and so on. The customers were being educated on manners – and they didn't mind.

Yagnanarayana's penchant for novelty found expression in MTR's food as well. Rava idli, one of the star dishes, was invented because of the shortage of rice during World War II. The recipe for bisibele bath, another bestseller, that the restaurant still follows was improvised by him, says Hema, who points out that the original Mysore dish is a lot milder than the spicy MTR recipe. The audience lapped it up. So popular is the MTR version of the bisibele bath that a person who has eaten this may be excused for believing that it is the 'authentic' version. There were also innovations such as ice cream with a mix of canned fruit. This again became an iconic MTR dish and still sells well. In fact, recipes for sambar, khara bath and other star dishes associated with MTR were all improvisations eventually standardized by Yagnanarayana.

All these are thought of as 'traditional' dishes today, but in his time they were inventive.

In 1968, Yagnanarayana Maiya passed away, handing over the mantle to his nephew Harishchandra Maiya, Hema's father, and the legacy continues with the third generation in the saddle today. (Yagnanarayana's son Sadananda Maiya, who had started building up the range of ready-to-eat foods around the time of the Emergency, got that part of the business in 1994, when the company was divided. He sold off MTR Foods to Orkla, a Norwegian company, in 2007 for $80 million. He and his family went on to launch Maiya's, another brand of ready-to-eat food with similar products, as well as restaurants under the Maiya's brand name.)

Today, as the third-generation owners go about trying to cautiously expand the original MTR restaurant brand, they are clear that nostalgia is their USP. Hema is candid when she tells me that while it is impossible to recreate the Lalbagh Road ambience at other outlets, they try to tell the history of the iconic brand through story boards and various touchpoints in the consumer experience. And there is no tampering with the 'original' recipes, which are all now highly standardized.

Even in franchised-out international operations, intensive staff training is undertaken by the family and key cooks are always provided by the family. MTR restaurants follow a traditional hierarchy that is different from the way most restaurant kitchens are organized. Restaurant kitchens around the world, including in India, follow the French system with its structure of head chef, sous chef, line chefs and so on. In traditional Indian kitchens, however, typically one cook would specialize in cooking just one dish and was ranked according to how skilled their job required them to be. So, in a Lucknowi kitchen, a qorma cook would be senior to a masalchi or spice grinder or naanbhai, while in an Udupi kitchen, the sambar cook was deemed to be the most skilled professional. This is somewhat like a Japanese kitchen, where a sushi chef who undergoes years of training perfecting his craft is held in high esteem.

Wherever a new MTR restaurant opens in the world, the sambar cook is always sourced from the Maiya's home village of Parampalli, as are one or two other key cooks. The family is in touch with the families of these cooks and Hema tells me that the first thing they do when they visit any of their restaurants is to enquire about the well-being of the families. This close connection with their cooks and community is necessary to ensure that the taste of dishes is maintained. In short, the brand value at MTR is authenticity backed by tradition. In fact, Hema and her bothers have decided not to have franchises within India and not to accept private equity money, in order to maintain full creative control over their restaurants.

The brand today does not want to innovate or change its core product – even though, ironically, as we have seen, its founders always kept innovating and much of the newness they introduced in the early years of the 20th century is what made MTR.

But are these two values of tradition and innovation contradictory? And is the MTR family doing the right thing by so scrupulously sticking to the old ways? The answer to the latter in my opinion is a firm yes. If we analyse how the audiences have changed, we realize that what is deemed traditional and heritage today is a novelty for audiences who have either heard of the legend of MTR food but not tasted it (in case of different geographies) or a newer generation within Bengaluru which has no nostalgia for the old MTR. The city today is a melting pot of immigrants – all these people don't really know MTR, but they come because they buy into the story of nostalgia. Sticking to heritage, in fact, is then a marketing tool. Traditional is new because the audience is new.

When MTR was coming up as Brahmin Coffee Club, on the other hand, its audience was more restricted. Its patrons were largely already acquainted with the kind of food being served by the small restaurant. It was convenience dining initially – as exemplified by the story of the 'car service'. To turn this convenience dining into experience-led dining, innovation was needed to create something that would be a little different from what was available at home – but not so different as to alienate an audience that was neither diverse nor cosmopolitan. MTR got it right then. It continues to get it right now. Restaurants need to understand their audiences at the end of the day – that's where most brands go wrong. Those who get it right are richly rewarded.

Sagar Ratna: Why brands must not tamper with their 'soul'

Those of us who grew up in the late 1980s and '90s in Delhi have a nostalgia for Sagar Ratna, the brand of tiffin-style Udupi restaurant associated with rava masala dosas, with dahi vadas that don't seem to lose their crispiness when dipped in the sweetened yoghurt, with the 'red' onion–tomato chutney that Delhiites were not used to eating till the Defence Colony restaurant made it popular, and more. We all also have an image of Jayaram Banan welcoming us at the door personally in our heads. Banan, a runaway-kid-turned-restaurateur, set up Sagar Ratna in the mid-1980s and built his fortune on its success. He went on to open several outlets throughout the NCR and some more in smaller towns in northern India. And he has another successful brand, Swagath, serving Mangalorean-style seafood, right next to Sagar in Defence Colony.

In 2011, about two and a half decades since he opened the first outlet, Banan sold a 77 per cent stake in Sagar Ratna to Mumbai-based private equity fund India Equity Partners for approximately ₹138 crore. The result was disastrous. Almost immediately, the two partners in the business found that they were at odds with one another and did not see eye to eye on many major issues, including operations and product, according to industry rumours. Neither of the parties have ever gone on record to say what the problem was.

But there were problems aplenty. In 2016, I met both Banan and Murali Krishna Parna, who had been brought in by the investing fund to be the CEO of the company in 2013, and who was going about cleaning up operations, stemming the bleeding by shutting down outlets as well as introducing innovative 'younger' products in order to find a new, younger audience and with an aim to also scale up Sagar Ratna.

He spoke to me about mini idlis on satay sticks, dosa rolls like frankies, cheese dosas to appeal to pizza-munching munchkins whose parents may want the traditional masala dosa, 'so that there is something for everyone'. I sampled some of the new products in his company and frankly they struck terror in my heart. My beloved dosa place was turning into some kind of an Americanized QSR, I thought. There is, after all, something called cultural appropriation, and inventiveness does not mean that cultural nuances be sacrificed, in my view.

A day after meeting Parna, by some quirk of fate, I ran into Banan, who still closely monitored his Swagath business. He refused to say anything on the subject of Sagar and souring relations, but just ominously said, 'We'll get everything back on track, you wait and watch.'

A few months later, in 2017, Banan did indeed buy back his entire stake from the fund. Although there was no official confirmation from either party, the buzz was that he had bought it at a discounted price at which it had been sold earlier.[6] Today, he is back in business. He has sworn off any funding options, but wants to grow the company to 100 company-owned outlets in the next five years, and an equal number of franchised stores across the country. (At the time of writing this, Sagar Ratna has 95 outlets, of which 36 are company-owned.)

We don't know how successful Banan will be in this bid to scale up. Yet, what this disastrous attempt at giving up control in a bid to grow, and in the process allowing the core of the restaurant to be tampered with, shows us is that individualistic restaurants which are built around the idea of food and have created a brand around that cannot really become assembly-line productions. The moment you want to be something for everyone, peddling pizzas in dosa diners, you lose not just your audience but your brand equity.

HOW CHEFS CAN BE RESTAURATEURS

Ritu Dalmia, Riga Foods, and
Regi Mathew, Kappa Chakka Kandhari

RESTAURATEURS OFTEN ARE WARY of building up chefs as brands because there often comes a point when chefs want either a larger chunk of the business (which restaurateurs may feel is unfair, given that a restaurant requires many things other than just food to set up and sustain themselves) and an equity stake or want to leave, lured by better prospects. For a creative chef who wants to build a long-standing brand, this is a dilemma. They must be happy to be a salaried employee; if they want greater control and larger rewards from the business, then the only other long-term option is to set up their own restaurant.

However, to be a chef in charge of the creativity in the kitchen as well as a restaurateur driving the business is no mean task. It is a balancing act that leaves people burnt out for obvious reasons. Take a simple scenario: As a talented chef, you may want to create dishes in a way that is not viable commercially. You may want to experiment with cuisines and ingredients and techniques but find you are not in sync with the market in which your restaurant is operating. As a restaurateur, your job would be to connect with the right market, to safeguard profit, and also to keep any creative hubris in check – to take into account audience tastes and what is acceptable to them. A restaurant, after all, is a business and not a personal passion project. Business and passion can and do marry, but there are jobs at stake and the financial responsibility that comes with running an enterprise.

It is hard for an individual to be able to resolve the conflict between creative experimentation with financial necessities. We have examples of chefs who have almost entirely turned into marketing executives for their restaurants and we have examples of chefs who cannot market their restaurants and run the business at all. To be able to achieve a happy median is rare and tough.

Chef-restaurateurs Ritu Dalmia and Regi Mathew, however, have walked this tightrope better than most in the country – not sacrificing their creativity at the altar of commerce, but also running commercially viable restaurants.

Dalmia is one of India's most talked about chefs and not just because she is so bravely outspoken on issues that are close to her heart. She was, for instance, one of the petitioners for striking down Section 377 of the Indian Penal Code and has been an LGBT rights champion. Dalmia's personality has always been forceful.

Even when she was first starting out, she was not one to mince words, telling customers off if they didn't like the pasta al dente, refusing to pander to those who didn't want to eat the Italian dishes the way they are meant to be and putting things on the menu that she believes in. She is passionate and forceful about seeking out the best quality ingredients for her restaurant, actively pursuing suppliers to get what she wants, and she is known to never skimp on paying top rupee.

In short, she does not compromise on her convictions and that comes across in her personality and on her plates. These traits of fierce independence, of willingness to stick your neck out to pursue what you believe in and passion are, however, balanced by an innate Marwari conservatism when it comes to spending money on the 'superfluous'. Unlike many newbie restaurateurs who splurge on the interiors and fancy equipment, Dalmia is known to behave like a prudent homemaker budgeting for necessities – making do with basic decor and equipment whose wear and tear is not going to cost her the earth, as she confesses. I totally get this kind of old-fashioned thrift, as would many Indians who grew up in a less consumerist society.

What this trait helps Dalmia do is balance her budget. Her food costs may be higher than most other restaurants' in her genre, but she is able to open a restaurant for far less investment than many rivals. The cautious approach to money is also reflected in avoiding private equity funding, despite having created a brand like Diva almost two decades ago. I have had this conversation with Dalmia many times, and she has always told me how she does not understand the valuation game and does not subscribe to it. Her business sense is more solidly conventional – a restaurant is viable if you control cost and make a profit, and each unit has to be viable. She looks at the bottom line closely.

In 2016, industrialist Analjit Singh, a long-standing patron at Diva, decided to invest in Dalmia's Riga Foods, till then a partnership company jointly owned by Dalmia and entrepreneur Gita Bhalla. Now, Singh owns 51 per cent of the business, while the remainder is split between Dalmia and Bhalla. Dalmia says this infusion of corporate money into her highly personal and till-then idiosyncratic business (in many ways, as I see it) has helped by providing structure and also because now there are people to take care of the backend, while she does her thing creatively.

However, from my observation, Riga Foods is still very much a personalized enterprise. One day, when I was talking to Dalmia about her expansion plans in Europe – she had opened two restaurants in Milan, Spica, a multi-cuisine restaurant, and Cittamani, which is an Indian restaurant, and an Italian one outside London in a boutique hotel bought by Singh, who was extending his hospitality portfolio – she took a break for a cigarette and to call Singh, who wanted to know some details about one of the menus! Clearly, this was not the usual relationship between an investor and chef-restaurateur; here the investor seemed almost as passionate as the founder of the business – always a recipe for more soulful, personalized restaurants.

Riga Foods now plans to go to Tier-II cities in continental Europe with Cittamani, which is Dalmia's take on modern Indian food with Italian accents – pizza fritta fashioned from a kachori, for instance, stuffed with peas. Then there is tagliolini with kurkuri bhindi, risotto with Hyderabadi baingan ka salan, besides more straightforward renditions of traditional regional Indian dishes. Despite the ambitious plans and the fact that with the infusion of capital Dalmia can now afford to expand in Europe, something that no Indian restaurant company has done before, her personality and style of thinking up restaurants and executing them remains the same. 'Everyone told me not to do the first Cittamani in Milan because Italians don't like Indian food and they will not pay the kind of price we are commanding (€60 for dinner, which is at least 30 to 40 per cent more expensive than regular Indian tandoori places in Europe). I was told to look at London because that is a more evolved market for Indian food. But you know me...' Dalmia trailed off.

It is an admission of sheer obstinacy, the forceful will to do something that no one has attempted before because she believes in the idea. This is the only way she knows of working, and that is what makes her tick. Without this personality, she wouldn't be who she is and certainly her restaurants would not even exist.

Dalmia has been lucky, or perhaps astute, to have found a business partner in Singh, one who is giving her the space to express herself freely through her restaurants and food while still handholding her through the intended expansion of the company. My belief is that this is the ideal arrangement for passion-led chef-restaurateurs, whose personalities are so forceful that they can only see their vision and no one else's. A private fund interested primarily in increasing valuations and not led by passion per se could never have worked as investors/partners for Dalmia.

Chef Regi Mathew in Chennai is in a similar situation. Mathew, who was born in Kottayam, started his career as a Thai chef with the Taj but discovered that it was a passion for a rediscovery of his own culinary roots that drove him. He started consulting for the Chennai-based Oriental Cuisines group and opened Ente Keralam for them in 2010, a restaurant based on solid research into the micro-regional cuisines of Kerala; dishes from small regions, recipes sometimes cooked by just a single family. As a consultant, Mathew had set up many different kinds of restaurants, but when his personal story, his passion and his work finally met, the result was stupendously successful.

The Ente Keralam chain across Chennai and Bengaluru put food from Kerala on the fine-dining map for the first time, and was a huge hit. Mathew's research into traditional recipes, utensils and cooking techniques from his state had all been incorporated into the restaurant and diners saw it as a hugely 'authentic' project, immediately identifying with it – even if they had never had that kind of food before.

Ente Keralam got both kinds of audiences. People from

the state living away from home, nostalgic about non-touristy, genuine flavours, and those who were keen to experiment and explore. Mathew ran the enterprise closely, and a big part of his success was building a chain from a fine-dining restaurant, but one still very focused on food. To standardize recipes, develop supply chains and have enough staff to cook authentically is always a challenge if a speciality restaurant decides to expand. Mathew was able to manage it. Yet, he did not own the brand (restaurateur M. Mahadevan, who owns the Copper Chimney restaurants, Hot Breads and Oriental Cuisines restaurants group in Chennai, is the owner) and had to leave it ultimately.

In 2018, he set up the second such detailed brand – this time co-owned by him. Kappa Chakka Kandhari in Chennai is the 100th restaurant that he has set up, but the first where part of the investment is his own (the rest by two of his friends, John Paul and Augustine Kurian). Once again, it is Kerala and its various micro-cuisines that drive Mathew, now a chef-restaurateur. Kappa Chakka Kandhari has unique recipes sourced from various villages in the state and steers away from the usual appams, stew and Malabar parottas. Instead, it has elusive recipes such as Ramassery idli (from the Ramassery region) steaming in a cloth over a claypot (its uniqueness lies in this unusual way of steaming), home dishes like pathiri (rice crepes) and a fish curry cooked by a 68-year-old grandmother who has been employed full-time at the restaurant to cook just that one dish.

The dishes took three years to research, and there was a further gestation period when Mathew started off with pop-ups in the UAE and Bengaluru, besides Chennai, to test the waters. Needless to say, something like this can only be built when the chef is very closely linked to the entire product, and following this particular business model of friendly investments – with Mathew still firmly in charge. He is confident of scaling up the brand, and given his success with Ente Keralam, you do think that even such a restaurant with so much detailing can perhaps go to at least a couple of other cities.

However, because it is so heavily personality-led, so individualistic and centred around a love for a specific culture – just as Ritu Dalmia's restaurants tend to be – there is a limit to how much the format can be scaled up. The question to ask, therefore, is how far restaurant companies helmed by strong chefs can grow, beyond a few outlets closely monitored by the chef and which reflect their personal sensibilities. Is there another way that Dalmia and Mathew can build a bigger restaurant company – where the number of outlets can scale up but the soul is still intact?

Any chef-led, food-driven restaurant brand has a challenge when it comes to scaling – for one, it is a business that depends on an individual chef's brand, even if the cooking is done by head chefs of every outpost and not the executive chef; establishing consistency and the same kind of food that patrons come to expect from the reputation of the original outlet is challenging, creating SOPs, finding the right ingredients in far-flung outposts, finding enough bandwidth to execute all of these, and getting the right franchise players and working with them are almost insurmountable barriers. Even internationally, restaurant brands led by famous chefs who have built huge empires straddling continents have grappled with this difficulty, even if we don't hear about it. In Singapore, last year, the Lion City's only three-Michelin-star restaurant, the eponymous Joel Robuchon had to shut ostensibly because of a location that didn't work, the apparent difficulty in finding enough customers for luxury restaurants, coupled with the high costs of rent, power and imported ingredients; additionally, such restaurants built around a personality sometimes forget other aspects of restaurateuring, such as service, the art of communicating the product, and efficiency, according to various media reports, including an incisive analysis by the *Singapore Business Review*, quoting chefs and industry insiders.[7]

However, when we look at some restaurant companies in other markets, there are interesting models at play.

No one has been more successful as a chef-restaurateur in North America than David Chang, the creator of the path-breaking restaurant brand Momofuku. Anyone who has ever seen even one episode of *Chef's Table* or videos of his interviews realizes that Chang's is a strong personality. He curses, he is direct, aggressive and does not tread lightly. And customers do expect this colourful personality to translate into the food at his restaurants as well. As an article in the *New York Times* by restaurant critic Pete Wells noted, 'civility is not part of the Momofuku brand'.[8]

Wells points out how though diners insist on seeing him as the creator of every scrap of food sold under his brand, Chang is a skilled restaurant operator, skilled at creating conditions for his chefs to come up with food that is not only novel but relevant to those markets.

Chang today is at the centre of a restaurant empire, with his company Momofuku owning 10 sit-down restaurants in three countries. He is also part-owner of Milk Bar, a chain of haute bakeries, as well as seven outlets of Fuku, a chain of quick-service chicken counters. Then there are noodle bars and a new counter-service restaurant concept in New York called Bang Bar. That makes Chang an incredible restaurateur as well as a talented and hugely successful chef. How has he managed this dual role?

The answer to that is important for chefs like Dalmia and Mathew. Chang has not only collaborated with and invested in quirky smaller-format, scalable models, but as his fine-dining restaurants show, he also has an eye for nurturing talented chefs who have their own voice and put their own individuality on the platter in their tasting menus, and yet think closely enough to be part of the larger Momofuku ethic.

If you examine Chang's public personality, a strong sense of individualism, of a rebellious temperament willing to go against the grain, emerges. This defines his food. But it also forms the underpinning of his restaurants – they are diverse, yet united by a way of looking at food that pushes the envelope and challenges stereotypes. What also unites them is the attention to detail that is the hallmark of any top-class restaurant, a quality that is evident in the cooking as well as the service and the entire look and feel of a restaurant. Chang, as an excellent chef, obviously wouldn't be where he is without that kind of attention to the finer details in his food, however no-fuss and non-pompous it is.

It is this same quality of balance between simplifying by stripping away the frills and giving a top-notch, comfortable yet chic service experience to his customers that now comes through all his restaurants. The chef and the restaurateur can coexist in the same mind. But it does take a special one to be able to be both simultaneously and consistently.

The making of Gaggan Anand's empire

Chef Gaggan Anand is undisputedly the most successful Indian chef and restaurateur – even though it is in Bangkok and not in India that he found success. Anand, who grew up in Kolkata, and had a frustrating stint working in Indian hotels, something that he never minces words about, went to Bangkok with just about $500 in his pocket and his dreams of making it big a little over a decade ago. Anand's restaurant company, in which he was a minority shareholder, made $24 million annually, as he told me in an interview, while at the peak of its success. Half of this revenue came from his eponymous restaurant Gaggan, he said, the restaurant where he did Indian food with modern presentations, emoji-only menu, eaten without cutlery.

In August 2019, Anand shut Gaggan in a bitter parting with his investors, as he revealed in an Instagram post on 19 August. According to this, in June, Anand had announced his resignation from the restaurant, which was followed by the resignation of his 65 team members from the restaurant in July. On 25 August, the restaurant closed its doors permanently[9] in what seems to be a bitter parting with the majority shareholders of the company. In his three-page Instagram post, Anand promised his patrons that he will now open a new restaurant in Bangkok with his team by October 2019, where he was to be a solo owner, with his baby daughter Tara as the majority shareholder. Before all of this, Anand had planned to open an ultra-luxury 16-seater restaurant in Fukuoka, Japan, within a small hotel built on an entire hillside.

Anand's story, or as much of it as we know, seems to be yet another example of the tensions that exist between restaurateurs and chefs who become brands. Before the fallout, Anand had told me how he was investing in the businesses of his protégés, such as the Suhring brothers (Suhring Bangkok) and Garima Arora (Gaa, Bangkok). Arora confirmed to me that Gaggan owns a 20 per cent stake in the restaurant along with Garima and three others, who all own similar stakes. Anand also has investments in Meatlicious (a grills-only restaurant) and Mihara Tofuten (a tofu-only restaurant).

This then was a restaurateuring strategy similar to David Chang's, where the idea was to create individualistic restaurants led by talented chefs under one umbrella.

THE BIG DADDY OF INDIAN FOOD RETAIL

Anjan Chatterjee, Speciality Restaurants

IN MUMBAI, JUST AS I have finished talking to him about the business of restaurants, Anjan Chatterjee is anxious to know the exact time of my flight back to Delhi the next morning. He calculates the time when I am supposed to check out of the hotel and tells me that he will have a box of sandesh delivered to me just around that time. That way, I will be able to take back the freshest possible mithai that he wants me to try from a special shop that he loves. It is indeed some of the best nolen gur sandesh that I have ever eaten – including what I've bought from shops in Kolkata.

You can't not be taken in by the large-hearted Bengali-ness of Chatterjee, or Dada, as he is known by all and sundry in the hospitality business. You cannot also discount the warmth and passion for food that define his personality and that continue to drive him even after 25 years in a relentless business.

Chatterjee, the restaurateur, has had many highs and lows. The business of restaurants, after all, can be started with passion but passion alone is not enough to sustain such a long innings at the helm of one of India's largest networks of premium and casual dining restaurants (58 outlets across different brands at the time of writing) and the only Indian restaurant company in the non-QSR space to have gone public (in 2012). But as I hear the oft-repeated story of how Chatterjee and his wife started out by entertaining foodie friends at their 1 BHK house in Mumbai (she did the cooking, following her family's East Bengal recipes) before starting a tiny 32-cover Bengali, fish-only restaurant in Colaba called Only Fish in the early 1990s, and then the first Mainland China in quick succession at Saki Naka, it becomes clear that along with a passion for food that all Bengalis purportedly have, Chatterjee has also had one extra quality that most Bengalis will profess to not have – ambition.

Bengali food may be his passion – best represented perhaps by his brand Oh! Calcutta – but Chatterjee's ambition to be a noteworthy restaurateur with a nationwide footprint resulted in the inception of Mainland China in 1995. Right from its very start, the idea was to go to multiple locations and build it into a chain. The inclination towards Chinese food may have come from Kolkata's Chinese restaurants, but Chatterjee wanted a restaurant that would serve 'real Chinese food', dim sum, Peking duck et al., to the middle class in the late 1990s and the early 2000s, when this kind of food was hard to find at best.

Chatterjee had already worked in the media, hotel and advertising industries by the time he conceptualized the brand (he ran his own advertising agency) and soon after the Saki Naka outlet, he opened Mainland China in Bengaluru, going against conventional wisdom that says that a restaurateur must expand within one zone to be operationally sound, achieve perfect standardization and control cost, rather than go into an entirely different geography.

It was a risky move, but it paid off. Chatterjee stuck to the south for a while after that, before heading north and east. Today, Mainland China is his biggest brand – pegged as a premium casual concept – and accounts for about 45 per cent of the business of Speciality Restaurants, Chatterjee's company.

In 2012, Speciality Restaurants went public. It's come a long way since, going debt-free (from a total debt of ₹42 crore before the IPO) and has money in the bank to fund expansion (at the time of writing). Yet there are challenges. Pressure from a private equity investor in the company that had held on even after the IPO apparently forced the company to expand haphazardly and too fast, according to an *Economic Times* report,[10] adding outlets when it did not necessarily have the bandwidth. This put pressure on the balance sheet and profits. Chatterjee is in the process of correcting some of this – he is closing some outlets, renegotiating rents and tweaking the product in different markets. Among other issues that dog the business, such as changing consumer preferences over the years, what Speciality perhaps also did not get was enough patient capital to sustain and sustainably expand a large chain operation. And therein lies the group's and Chatterjee's biggest learning, as he told me once in a conversation.

When a restaurateur is pushed to grow too fast, they begin to lose their personal touch with every store, which means that everything from staffing to rent to product is no longer looked into deeply by the restaurateur whose personality and personal sense of the business had led to the concept's success in the first place. Fine-dining restaurants and those described as premium casual – basically experience-led restaurants – struggle when restaurateurs cannot monitor the business themselves.

The store-level economics – which should be the top priority of any business – suffer, and in the end the company slips. Restaurant companies cannot be sustained by passion alone, but if personalization and passion are key to an experience-led restaurant brand, how far can you afford to let them go? It is a conundrum that hardly anyone seems to have got right in the Indian restaurant space for now.

When Anjan Chatterjee started Mainland China, a model that inspired him, he says, was PF Chang's – the American-Chinese restaurant chain started in 1993 by Paul Fleming and Philip Chiang. In 2012, the private equity firm Centerbridge Partners bought the brand in a deal that valued the chain at $1.1 billion. In 2019, the PE firm sold the brand to TriArtisan Capital Partners and Paulson & Co.[11] PF Chang's has more than 210 outlets in the US plus 95 restaurants in more than 25 countries around the world, according to its website, at the time of writing.

As part of the sale, *Bloomberg* reported, all of the company's more than $675 million of total debt will be taken out at par. The chain had been burdened with heavy debt as well as stiff competition in the saturated US restaurant market, where food prices have been on the decline.

Though PF Chang's found a new buyer, the debt burden it carried prior to the sale is a sobering reminder about the nature of the restaurant business. Building a big chain has massive pressures, with the seemingly impossible tasks of finding adequate human resources for every outlet, maintaining consistency, finely calibrating the product in every market, and remaining cognizant of every small change in rapidly changing consumer preferences.

Anjan Chatterjee's father, a research scientist with middle-class values, measured wealth by one parameter, as the restaurateur told me: whether one was debt-free or not. Speciality has tried to maintain this value, Chatterjee says. However, today's wealth-creation models are different, with restaurateurs ignoring the bottom line for increased valuations. We will talk in detail about this scaling-up conundrum in a later section.

Advice to new restaurateurs

One of the first things Anjan Chatterjee will tell you should you ask him for his advice as a restaurateur who has been around for a quarter-century is to 'kill your ego'. Till date, Chatterjee does not enter his restaurant's kitchens without asking the chef in charge for permission. In a business where people are so important, it is important to respect everyone and listen to everyone, whether it is the wait staff or your own son who is training to take over.

Second, store economics are very important. Rent should

not be allowed to go beyond 10–12 per cent of revenue, he says, or your bottom line suffers. A restaurant should be able to recover its investment in two and a half years, else you must shut it. Similarly, it is important to constantly innovate on the product, especially if the brand is an old one. Concepts and food offerings get outdated very fast otherwise, says Chatterjee.

The biggest and most valuable piece of advice, however, was on expansion. The more you expand, the thinner you spread and the more difficult it gets. So, consolidate yourself first, develop consistency in the product and find skilled manpower (which is tough to come by) before you look at expansion. A restaurant company's profitability is what is most important at the end of the day – whether it has 20 restaurants or 200 under its belt.

SLIPPING UP AND GETTING UP

Ashish Kapur, Yo! China, and Rahul Akerkar, Qualia

AT THE AGE OF 27, Ashish Kapur decided to build an Indian McDonald's. Yo! China was born because Kapur, an engineer with a mechanical, mathematical bent of mind, was fascinated by scale, as he told me once. In the early 2000s, Chinese food, or at least Indian-Chinese, was inordinately popular, and people loved to snack on chowmein, chilli chicken and the like as comfort food. But the only ones selling Chinese in this kind of quick format were the van guys, halwai shops and stalls, all in the unorganized segment. Then there were the hotel restaurants with completely different formats, but nothing in between.

Kapur's brainwave was to brand simple Indian-Chinese, present it in attractive boxes and combos and sell it out of shiny stores at a price that the young casual diner spent on a McDonald's burger. The enterprising Kapur managed to raise first ₹70 lakh from three angel investors to open the first outlet in 2003, and subsequently ₹25 crore from Matrix Partners, a private equity fund, in 2006, and then he and his partners went all-India in a 'spray' approach – stores spread across the country, not concentrated in a single geographic area.

With so much money at his disposal and a board comprised of much older and experienced professionals, Kapur found himself out of depth, he told me. He was being forced to expand rapidly, he felt, and taking decisions on the advice of 50-year-olds, against his own gut instinct. At its peak, by 2008, Yo! China had 60 outlets (McDonald's had 90 at that time in India), Kapur says, of which 40 per cent were franchises, with annual sales of ₹65 crore.

Those of us who were around and eating out then roughly know what happened next. The brand began slipping in the process of indiscriminate expansion. It didn't have the operational bandwidth to ensure quality and consistency, franchisees began doing their own thing, and the final nail in the coffin was the emergence of food courts in malls.

Overnight, what had been a novelty was now available for even cheaper at the food courts in shiny, red plastic trays. The concept was no longer aspirational and stores in the metros in upmarket locations began to lose customers. In the Tier-II cities, franchise owners were playing havoc with the product, serving all kinds of mishmash, and it lost credibility and reputation.

Then, Lehman Brothers happened. In its aftermath, Kapur and partners found themselves with ₹70 crore in debt, according to Kapur. The brand was losing ₹2 crore a month and there were bank loans to service. Kapur had ₹1.25 crore in his bank account and fat salaries to pay.

'I went bankrupt,' he told me, 'at such a young age, in my early 30s.' This was the wake-up call he needed. He called the board members to his house for a party, fed them well, served them expensive whisky, and at the end of the evening fired everyone. Kapur's wife Meghana still jokes that when they have to let anyone go, they call them home for a nice dinner first! The struggle to rebuild his life and career as a restaurateur had just begun.

I have known Kapur since just before crisis hit Yo! China. I was at the *Business Standard*, had witnessed his meteoric rise, and had proposed to do a 'Lunch with Business Standard' with him. That was a column in the paper where editors and writers invited an entrepreneur or CEO to a meal and then spoke to them about the industry and their personal journey, interspersing it with their own commentary and observations.

Kapur was a fantastic subject. I had invited him for a meal to Spice Route at the luxurious Imperial Hotel in Delhi, with the intention of drawing a tongue-in-cheek contrast between what Yo! China was selling ('McChowmein') and famous chef Veena Arora's Thai dishes. In fact, through the meal, I even asked him a pointed question as to how he would compare a chicken dish we had ordered with Yo! China's chilli chicken. Much to my delight, Kapur answered that he thought Yo! China was doing an equally good job with the dish as what had emerged out of this very pricey restaurant kitchen. I was suitably snide about that remark and had some fun at Kapur's expense, but he apparently didn't mind it at all and was very good-natured about it.

We kept in sporadic touch, but it was only when Yo! China was in trouble and Kapur was attempting to rework the brand that I got to know him much better and understand the core of his personality. Kapur was attempting to change Yo! China's brand promise – from a 'value' product which was no longer unique to high-quality Asian food. I had just come back from Thailand after doing a short cooking course and Kapur wanted me to curate a Thai menu for a food festival that would run as a special offering for a few months across select flagship outlets.

I roped in a Thai home cook I knew, and together, we spent considerable time training Yo! China's chefs and doing the menu. Kapur and his partners came for every tasting, and I discovered a restaurateur who seemed to be seeking increased sophistication all round compared to what he had started out with.

In fact, a key to Kapur's personality is indeed this desire to better himself, this constant search for sophistication. He travels frequently, is interested in new experiences and in gaining knowledge about not just restaurant models that are successful, but in his now core products like whiskies and wines, by constantly engaging with experts. It is a constant movement towards personal and professional betterment.

This growing sophistication and the desire to constantly seek out quality and luxury is reflected in the kind of restaurants Kapur and his partners have attempted in the wake of Yo! China. Gone are the massy underpinnings – the company today is firmly in the upscale bar and restaurants space, with concepts such as The Wine Company/The Wine Rack, Whisky Samba and Antares. They are all bars, but they all work because they tap into a middle-class Indian aspiration to be stylish and 'cool', similar to Kapur's own personal journey.

Wine was already starting to become cool in the metros when Kapur decided to make it more affordable through The Wine Company/The Wine Rack (he started retailing labels at lower prices than at the five-star bars) to the younger crowd, who would want to sip it recreationally, rather than be ruled by complicated rules, vintages and chateaux. With whisky, he did the opposite. Entry-level whiskies were sold at higher prices and more expensive ones at lower to encourage a more sophisticated crowd at the bar for a liquor that every Indian male of a certain age drinks. Then there were whisky cocktails designed to encourage women and millennials, who were interested in the bar category but weren't traditional Scotch drinkers.

Obviously, these are high-end concepts that have limited scalability. But the idea actually seems to be to create diverse brands in this space rather than scale up a single one. Kapur and his partners are in a space where aspiration drives their business instead of the mass appeal that they had sought to harness at the beginning. This, I believe, is more in sync with their personalities. They are serious players in the luxury/upscale casual dining space in the country because of this. The growth of each of their company's brands is funded by private accruals and private investments. Kapur, after all, had learnt an early lesson about such funding.

Chef-restaurateur Rahul Akerkar too burnt his hand with PE money. As most people in the Indian food business already know, in 2015, Akerkar found himself quitting his own company. Two decades ago, Akerkar started Degustibus Hospitality when he had come back from the US to set up the path-breaking restaurant Indigo in Colaba, Mumbai, which did casual, loosely 'Western' food with local ingredients, Akerkar's unique inventive style.

Indigo went on to be one of India's iconic restaurants before it finally shut in 2017, much after Akerkar had lost control of his business. The Colaba restaurant was never quite the same after the chef-restaurateur's exit. After all, Akerkar's stamp on its food, wine, service and easy charm had been intrinsic to the brand. Indigo Deli, the chain of more casual restaurants, on the other hand, continues to exist, and more outlets are being added by the owners of the business, who took creative as well as business control after Akerkar left.

Akerkar, on the other hand, is back to what he knows best: Setting up a restaurant that is chef-led, rather than P&L driven – as he told me once, if the restaurant as a product (and not just the food) is well run, numbers take care of themselves.

Qualia, which Akerkar opened in 2019, is funded with his own money and clearly it is a restaurant built with a lot of heart. Located in Mumbai's Lower Parel, it is, to my mind, the chicest, most cosmopolitan restaurant in the country today. It's not as if it is formal or 'stuck up'. Like Akerkar himself, there is warmth and a casual charm combined with an underplayed urbaneness that is hard to define but easy to feel when you step into the space.

The staff is chatty and converse with you with warmth and personalized interest, something that's missing from Indian restaurants in general. Akerkar, meanwhile, is everywhere – behind the bar, in the open kitchen (there is no back kitchen), looking after guests. His stamp is visible in every plate that combines flavours in fascinating ways, uses preservation techniques like fermentation and pickling, and integrates local ingredients and Maharashtrian influences from Akerkar's own upbringing in a unique manner, giving us food and an experience that can only be described as very 'international'.

Will Qualia go on to become a success and a long-standing brand? A key will be how it engages with its niche market – to my mind it is a niche restaurant, relatively expensive and offering high quality in a market cluttered by low-quality bars and restaurants where the price is low too. The sophistication that it demands from its audience also makes it niche. However, if Akerkar can be patient – because all niche upscale restaurants require tons of patience – he may make a credible success out of it. For the time being, the restaurant seems to be doing quite well and running full.

What is sure is that the restaurant shares Akerkar's and Indigo's DNA – quality and sophistication ahead of financials. Over eggs Kejriwal at the Willingdon Club one Mumbai summer, Akerkar had showed me the financial history of Indigo on his laptop, and he points out the various highs in numbers to me. 'In 2003, we were making ₹1.2 crore a month,' he said. 'In 2007, ₹2 crore a month in sales; in December that year, the average daily sales were ₹6 lakh.' In essence, it was a successful restaurant, whose top line was among the highest in the country at that time. This, he stressed, was achieved through good restaurateuring (food, service, experience) rather than chasing numbers. Perhaps at Qualia it will be the same.

THE GRAND DAME

Camellia Panjabi, MW Eat Group

WHEN IT COMES TO creating long-lasting restaurant brands, Camellia Panjabi is a legend. The former marketing head for the Taj group of hotels, Panjabi is responsible for creating some of the most iconic brands that have lasted well over four decades, and are still going strong. Each time you step into Golden Dragon for its Schezwan food, into the Sea Lounge in Mumbai or Machan in Delhi for street flavours recreated in a five-star, to the iconic Karavalli in Bengaluru for South Indian regional food, it is Panjabi's vision and handiwork that you are a part of.

A Cambridge graduate, Panjabi joined the Tatas in 1969. In 1971, she was moved to the Taj to look after sales, a job that she interpreted in a much larger sense. Cuisine was to be the way to drive revenue, and as part of hotelier Ajit Kerkar's team, Panjabi was soon redefining restaurants in India. At a time when everyone was serving Punjabi food, she decided to serve local regional cuisines in Tanjore, the Taj Mumbai's Indian restaurant (that lasted till 2001, when it was changed to the Masala series by Hemant Oberoi).

'When the chefs protested and said that they did not have the recipes to cook this kind of food, I decided to get into food research and give them recipes,' Panjabi reminiscences. With her formidable social contacts, she got the best classical Indian recipes from the royal homes in Rajasthan and Hyderabad, from Delhi society's movers and shakers and from simple housewives. 'When we were setting up Karavalli and wanted to do south Indian food, I went to lecture at the Dadar catering college and asked the young final-year students who was ready to go learn from housewives in their kitchens. Only Sriram Aylur raised his hand and we sent him all over to research in homes,' she says. The result was the best-researched south-western coastal food restaurant (at the Taj Gateway in Bengaluru) the country has ever had. Karavalli is legendary, and even today, a meal there is exceptional. Chef Naren Thimmaiah, who presides over its kitchens, is no less legendary, having been immersed in the cuisine for an incredible 30 years that he has spent at the restaurant. He personally checks ingredients every day (despite being the hotel's executive chef too), hires staff for the restaurant carefully – believing that regional recipes can only be truly replicated by cooks belonging to those cultures – and researches the cuisines of the south-west minutely himself. The culture of careful research that Panjabi started at the Taj by handpicking key people, and by her own example, is alive in a restaurant such as this and shows us how strong DNA is key to a brand.

Panjabi quit the Taj group in 2001 and joined her sister Namita, who had, together with her husband Ranjit Mathrani, set up Chutney Mary in London in 1989. Ranjit and Namita also bought Veeraswamy, London's oldest Indian restaurant, and refurbished it to serve high-end classical Indian food. Camellia was an informal adviser, but in 2001, she joined them formally and became a director in their company, jointly looking after cuisine with her sister, and in charge of marketing and conceptualizing restaurants – a job she knew well.

She was soon off the mark with Masala Zone, a regional Indian thali and street food restaurant in the affordable dining space. Today, there are multiple outlets of the brand all over London. Then came Amaya, a stylish and utterly chic grill restaurant, where the tandoor and the sigri occupy pride of place in the open kitchen, along with a salad section and a few complex curries. All these are among London's best-known Indian restaurants, much awarded and talked about, and all of them have been iconic brands for decades.

When I met Panjabi in London and spent a few days with her, eating at various restaurants together (high-quality dishes such as whole grilled-in-tandoor baby cauliflower sourced from a single field in France, Dover sole done delicately in the tandoor, the elusive Rajput safed maans, kothu parotta, chaat, squid tossed in coastal spices and so on), I learn that the MW Eat group, as it is called, with three luxury restaurant brands (Chutney Mary, Veeraswamy and Amaya) and six outlets of Masala Zone, is not just highly respected, but also the UK's most profitable Indian restaurant group at the moment.

It recorded an annual turnover of £27 million net of

VAT (value-added tax) in the year ending March 2018, and EBITDA of £5.6 million, or 20.8 per cent of revenue. This puts it far ahead of every Indian restaurant company operating in the UK in terms of profitability for the year. (In terms of turnover, the rapidly expanding Dishoom is bigger, with slimmer profit margins.)

According to a Plimsoll report on the UK restaurant industry released in June 2019, the company grew by 3 per cent in value over one year and was one of the top 50 fast-growing restaurant companies in the UK. No other Indian restaurant company was in the top 50 on the list.

All these are impressive numbers and bear testimony to the fact that long-lasting and iconic brands can be hugely profitable too.

So how did Camellia conceptualize the various brands? What were the reasons for her resounding success both in India and internationally, especially given the fact that Indian restaurant companies that seek to enter the London market often slip up? After my long discussions on various big-picture ideas with her, as well as after talking to her contemporaries like Habib Rehman, former ITC Hotels chief, I can analyse that her success is due to a gift for understanding her market and passion towards the product, as exemplified by the prodigious research and detailing that goes into all her restaurants.

'When you think of opening a restaurant, the first thing you must ask yourself is, why are you opening one and who will it cater to?' Panjabi says. She also minces no words when she tells me that she has always chased profits, not glory, which has been a by-product – the exact opposite of what she feels many restaurateurs do today. A brand is worth conceptualizing, she says, if one feels it can live for 30 to 40 years. 'How else will you make your money? In three to five years, a restaurant will barely return the investment, it is stupidity to again put in money into turning it into a new brand,' she says.

A long-lasting brand is obviously the result of passionate engagement, as we can see from the research that Panjabi put into each and every restaurant that she took up. She was equally devoted to studying her customers. When the Taj asked her to go to London because they wanted to set up operations there – including an Indian restaurant – Panjabi asked her boss Ajit Kerkar, who used to head the hotels business then, to let her stay in London for a year to assess the market. These were days of stiff foreign exchange restrictions, so she had to make do with a paltry daily allowance; nevertheless, she made sure to meet a variety of people, including chefs of other restaurants and the London media, travel widely and study customer behaviour. She conceptualized the Bombay Brasserie as a smart, upscale place serving regional Indian food and street food instead of the Punjabi-influenced heavy food served at the only two upscale Indian places in London at that time, Gaylord and Shezan.

Then, when the restaurant opened, for the first few months, she served as the hostess of the restaurant, listening to people when they came in to dine. 'My boss had told me that if you make a loss at the restaurant, we will have to shut it down because there was no way of sending money from the parent company to write these off, under FERA regulations, so I made sure that we were profitable,' she tells me.

Ever since then, the profitability of her restaurants has been paramount – even as she and her sister and brother-in-law continue to run these with passion, deeply involved in the day-to-day operations and with each of their erudite and cosmopolitan sensibilities stamped on to the design, the service and the very spirit of their enterprise.

PART 3

BY THE NUMBERS

Name of the Company		2016–17	2017–18
Speciality Restaurants Limited (Consolidated)	Turnover	312.42	296.79
	Net profit before tax	-28.95	-24.51
	Net profit after tax	-25.52	-46.77
Speciality Restaurants Limited (Standalone)	Turnover	312.42	296.79
	Net profit before tax	-25.28	-31.14
	Net profit after tax	-21.85	-53.40
BTB Marketing Private Limited	Turnover	77.44	
	Net profit before tax	-21.67	
	Net profit after tax	-21.67	
Impresario Entertainment and Hospitality Private Limited	Turnover	225.62	
	Net profit before tax	7.48	
	Net profit after tax	7.48	
Impresario Entertainment and Hospitality Private Limited (Consolidated)	Turnover	262.68	
	Net profit before tax	8.12	
	Net profit after tax	8.08	

(continued)

Name of the Company		2016–17	2017–18
Lite Bite Foods Private Limited	Turnover	144.04	185.08
	Net profit before tax	-46.08	-5.26
	Net profit after tax	-35.04	-2.88
Lite Bite Foods Private Limited (Consolidated)	Turnover	233.73	301.65
	Net profit before tax	-94.75	-47.54
	Net profit after tax	-79.79	-38.77
Massive Restaurants Private Limited	Turnover	130.50	160.56
	Net profit before tax	3.30	-12.74
	Net profit after tax	3.22	-14.25
Old World Hospitality Private Limited (Consolidated)	Turnover	171.35	
	Net profit before tax	6.22	
	Net profit after tax	2.71	
Old World Hospitality Private Limited	Turnover	105.08	101.83
	Net profit before tax	5.52	11.94
	Net profit after tax	3.70	8.98
Olive Bar and Kitchen (Consolidated)	Turnover	153.74	
	Net profit before tax	0.75	
	Net profit after tax	1.78	
Olive Bar and Kitchen (Standalone)	Turnover	149.95	
	Net profit before tax	0.69	
	Net profit after tax	1.77	
Riga Foods LLP	Turnover		24.18
	Net profit before tax		0.30
	Net profit after tax		0.10

Data obtained from the Ministry of Corporate Affairs website (http://www.mca.gov.in/mcafoportal/viewPublicDocumentsFilter.do) by the publisher
Figures in ₹ crore

The most popular brands and restaurateurs associated with each company:

- Speciality Restaurants: Mainland China, Oh! Calcutta, Sigree, Gong, Hoppipola
  Restaurateur: Anjan Chatterjee
- BTB Marketing: The Beer Café
  Restaurateur: Rahul Singh
- Impresario Entertainment and Hospitality: Social, Smoke House Deli
  Restaurateur: Riyaaz Amlani
- Lite Bite Foods: Punjab Grill, Tappa, Zambar
  Restaurateurs: Amit Burman, Rohit Aggarwal
- Massive Restaurants: Farzi Café, Papaya, Masala Library
  Restaurateur: Zorawar Kalra
- Old World Hospitality: Chor Bizarre, Comorin, Indian Accent, Tikka Town
  Restaurateur: Rohit Khattar
- Olive Bar and Kitchen: Olive, SodaBottleOpenerWala, Fatty Bao, Monkey Bar, Toast and Tonic
  Restaurateur: A.D. Singh
- Riga Foods: Diva, Cafe Diva
  Restaurateur: Ritu Dalmia

There is a lot of hype surrounding the restaurant universe, not just in India but all over the world. For the purpose of this book, however, we will limit our discussion to restaurants in India. The table at the beginning of this chapter shows the turnover and profit of some of the biggest restaurant companies in the country for the financial years ending 2018 and prior. These are companies that have shaped our restaurant culture, their brands are popular and their chefs celebrated on Instagram, Facebook and in the mainstream media every day.

Yet, as we can see from the numbers, many of the companies are struggling with profitability.

These are figures from the financial year ending 31 March 2018, but people in the industry, who spoke to me on condition of anonymity, give informal estimates that put the profitability of some of these companies even lower currently. In fact, they say that of the top Indian restaurant companies in the casual, premium casual or mixed-format segments, few are deemed to be profitable today.

There may be a few exceptions to this rule: Social's Hauz Khas outlet in Delhi, after a decade of existence, is reportedly making ₹1.9 crore in sales per month, on a rent of ₹11 lakh a month, leading to an EBITDA margin of more than 40 per cent, according to sources in the industry who did not want to be named. It pulls up the profitability of the entire company, obviously. But this is an exception.

In general, industry veterans like Sharad Sachdeva, formerly the CEO of the Amit Burman–promoted Lite Bite Foods, and who moved to heading operations of L Catterton, the private equity arm of French conglomerate LVMH, have this to say: If the store-level EBITDA margin of a restaurant is over 20 per cent, it is doing exceptionally well; if it is between 15 and 20 per cent, it is good; between 10 and 15 per cent is average; and less than 10 per cent is poor. Restaurant companies by and large calculate EBITDA or profits at a store level as well as at the corporate level, where profits from individual outlets are added and then the company's overheads deducted to give a measure of profitability (for a restaurant company which has multiple outlets, this is lower than store-level profitability). So, hypothetically, a company recording less than 5 per cent EBITDA margin at a store level would actually be making a loss at the overall corporate level. Also, it is important to consider here that any company that is in an expansion cycle may have higher depreciation costs factored in, and therefore, when anyone has to analyse the profitability of any restaurant company, it is important to look at store-level EBITDA.

Though industry insiders don't want to go on record, very few Indian restaurants today are making a store-level EBITDA margin of over 20 per cent, or even 15–20 per cent, across most of their stores. In fact, many companies are in the red because store-level profitability is very low – or non-existent.

To contrast this, I studied the financials and operations of MW Eat in London, owned by Ranjit Mathrani and Namita Panjabi, with Camellia Panjabi as a director. With highly acclaimed restaurants such as Chutney Mary, Amaya and Veeraswamy and seven outlets of a casual regional Indian concept Masala Zone, MW Eat was the most profitable Indian restaurant company in London in 2018. It registered an annual turnover of £27 million net of VAT and EBITDA at a corporate level of £5.6 million, a 20.8 per cent margin, for the year ending 31 March 2018. Its profit before tax margin was 15 per cent, according to a Plimsoll report.[1]

In general, the point to make here is that despite whatever the top line of any company, ultimately, it is the bottom line that indicates financial health.

In the years a restaurant group spends expanding and adding more outlets, it is natural for its profitability to be lower. Let me give you another point of comparison. Dishoom, the widely heralded company with a chain of Bombay-inspired restaurants across London (and now elsewhere in the UK), reported a jump in profit before tax from £0.9 million in 2017 to £2.3 million in 2018.[2] According to accounts filed with the UK's Companies House, turnover for 2018 stood at £44.9 million, up from £35.6 million the previous year, an increase of 26.3 per cent across its existing and new sites. Adjusted EBITDA was £4.3 million, against £2.2 million in 2017. Its adjusted EBITDA margin increased from 6.3 per cent to 9.6 per cent, while its gross profit margin increased from 31.4 per cent to 38.5 per cent.

Since it opened in 2010, the company has added seven outlets – five in London, one in Edinburgh and a new one in Manchester that came up in 2019. It also announced in July 2019 that it would be taking over the space adjacent to its Covent Garden restaurant – a former Jamie's Italian, with the restaurant to undergo a major redesign to mark its 10th anniversary.

The latest results, however, are also interesting because they show how a company even while expanding can continue to make reasonable profit.

Most Indian restaurant companies that are now owned in part or majority by private equity funds are also in the cycle of expansion, adding multiple outlets to various brands, which may put stress on the profit margins. However, there are other important factors weighing on profits, such as operational problems as a company expands, problems with management bandwidth and also customer fatigue with the brand once it loses its initial marketing-generated buzz. Finally, there is also the intrinsically fickle nature of the restaurant business itself, which is sensitive to all kinds of things – from seasonality and sentiment to changing or whimsical government policies.

PE funding is part of what many new entrepreneurs see as the 'wealth creation model', wherein funds invest in restaurant companies after assessing (i) the potential of the brand to scale, (ii) the personal credibility of the restaurateur/founder and the management team, (iii) unit economics, whether the restaurants are healthy and earning profits, and (iv) the concept that the restaurateur wants to scale up, and its potential to resonate with a large group of customers in varied markets. 'These are the most important things any PE fund sees when they want to invest in any company,' says Sachdeva.

A PE fund essentially treats any businesses it invests in, whether retail or restaurants, in a purely financial manner – their value must multiply, over a period of three, five or seven years, to be able to give returns to investors who have put money into the fund. Good returns would mean that the value of the company has multiplied substantially, and the fund is able to exit after selling its investment for several times the amount it invested. A bad investment obviously is when the restaurant company does not do well, the value of the brand does not increase as expected, or even declines, and the fund has to exit at little to no profit, or even a loss.

Naturally then, this model of PE-funded growth has risks associated with it, particularly since the restaurant business is uniquely sensitive, dependent as it is on the humans that run it and from whom it derives its custom, unlike most other retail or commodified industries.

In many parts of the world, including in mature markets such as London, we have seen casual dining chains come under great stress and several such as Jamie Oliver's crumble. Consequently, there have been criticisms levelled against PE funds, who sometimes may not have a grasp of the business, pressuring restaurants to grow despite a lack of bandwidth and fears of oversupply, leading to brands collapsing. Conversely, if you talk to PE funds you will find that many a time they point to the fact that restaurant operators themselves overpromise or under-deliver. What is fair to conclude is that in a sensitive business such as restaurants, if a restaurateur is seeking expansion through PE investment, there needs to be complete clarity and understanding on the deliverables and expectations, as well as a good working relationship between the representatives of the fund who sit on company boards (and often get involved in macro details) and the restaurant founder.

Restaurants need patient capital to grow. Take the case of Wagamama, the casual Asian chain acquired in 2018 by The Restaurant Group, a British company with several brands, in a whopping £559 million deal, from private equity fund Duke Street Capital.[3]

Duke Street Capital had bought the chain in 2011 for £215 million from Lion Capital and Graphite Capital, who jointly owned the business (Lion Capital in turn had acquired a 77.5 per cent stake from Graphite in 2005).

As you can see, Wagamama was fortunate, as were the funds that invested in it. It changed hands every six to seven years and did get patient capital to grow – in fact, it has been outperforming the casual dining market in the UK. And Duke Street Capital got fat returns on its investment.

In India, private equity is a relatively recent phenomenon when it comes to restaurants, and there haven't been any such spectacular exits to the best of my knowledge.

A lot of times, private equity funds seem less patient, restaurateurs point out – particularly when they don't own a large chunk of the business, or have bought a stake at a high valuation and thus look to exit quickly after recovering their investment. There are different types of funds, however, and different companies with different potential, so it is difficult to generalize, but as Sharad Sachdeva explained to me, 'If there is potential in a restaurant company, if the fund is convinced that it can grow the valuation substantially or the brand has the potential for an IPO, the fund will be inclined to wait for longer giving it the patient capital needed.'

A lot of times, this does not happen. Because the kind of fund that has invested in a business may not have deep pockets, may not really look at the restaurant space as a core area of its investments, may not have a clear understanding of the complex, people-led business that restaurants is and so on.

A lack of a clear working relationship with the restaurant brand's promoter/founder may translate into pressure the restaurant company may feel to grow at an unsustainable pace, adding outlets when clearly there is no capacity to grow while standardizing products and processes. This pressure may also create situations of oversupply in various markets, and brands land up opening outlets too close to each other, cannibalizing their own business. We shall examine these difficulties in scaling up when the company has PE investments in the next chapter.

Some restaurants choose to grow slowly and organically while still being family-owned companies. MW Eat (which is owned entirely by its founders) has added outlets over a 30-year window and has been able to sustain its brands for so long. It has managed in the process to retain its profitability.

For many individual restaurateurs, especially those whose ambition it may be to just create two to four outlets at most of every brand they own, this may be a better model to follow rather than taking in PE money with all its stresses and deliverables. However, even if you decide to build your brands and company like Camellia, Namita and Ranjit have done, there are problems unique to the Indian environment that you must be cognizant of.

According to hospitality consultant Samir Kukreja, a past

president of the NRAI, for a well-run restaurant company in India, even EBITDA at a corporate level of around 10 per cent is deemed good. However, many restaurateurs and industry insiders in private confess that few companies have been achieving that.

To determine the financial health of most restaurants in India is a tough task, with a lot of the business in the unorganized space, and where though 'white money' transactions have been increasing with stricter government policies, there are players yet to follow complete transparency. Several restaurant companies also operate as partnerships, for which taxation structures are different from those that apply to private limited companies. Additionally, disclosures about financial status are more difficult to track in the public domain for partnerships – especially since a single restaurateur may open multiple partnerships in different names in different cities, making it difficult for anyone to track their business.

Some restaurateurs hype up their numbers even when talking informally and off the record. A motivating factor for this, from my observations, could be because many work with partners/investors who are novices. People with no restaurant background often invest in the business for the social status it gives them – a restaurateur may find a bunch of such novices eager to pool in a couple of lakhs each to set up a restaurant.

Some restaurateurs I spoke with told me that they invest only if their calculations show 30 per cent profit at a store level and 18 months to recoup the capital expenditure, or capex. While exceptional restaurants may achieve this, more often than not, profits are much lower, and when you recover your investment depends on the restaurant model as well as how well the business is doing.

There are multiple challenges facing the restaurant business in India that a novice restaurateur must keep in mind. Of these, the most important is whether the concept itself is sustainable. Sometimes, restaurants are financially unviable because the very fundamentals are flawed. For instance, if a restaurant cannot work both its lunches and dinners optimally because of its location, or concept or any other challenge, it is obviously going to be unviable, using up expensive real estate while unable to earn optimally from it.

Then you have operational problems, often unforeseen, such as when chefs and restaurateurs do not devote enough time and attention to the business, which as we have discussed demands intense personal attention.

Or there may be problems between the partners or investors themselves, which ultimately lead to a brand shutting down. This is one of the most common reasons for restaurant failure. Then there are some common problems that every restaurant in this country faces that weaken the business potential of the entire sector.

It is a no-brainer that restaurants create jobs; they also have the capacity to boost tourism, as we have seen in so many regions in the world, from Spain to Singapore. According to the World Tourism Organization, one in every 11 jobs globally is created through tourism. Spain pitched itself as a gourmet destination and now gets some of the highest number of tourists annually – 82.6 million tourists in 2018.[4] India, in comparison, gets around 10 million visitors every year.[5]

Despite the huge benefits the restaurant industry can provide to the economy, employing people, enhancing tourism and bringing in revenue, there is as yet very little in the way of policy incentives for the industry. Urban planning in cities does not seem to take into account the need for dedicated spaces for neighbourhood restaurants and cafes. Every state has policies and licensing rules governing the business, and getting clearances is daunting to say the least. There are grey areas and scope for misuse of power, antiquated laws and irrational policies. All these are common complaints that you hear of from all restaurateurs. These drain an aspiring restaurateur mentally, physically and financially. In fact, very often I have come across people – especially women – who started off eagerly but realized that running a restaurant was not their cup of tea.

Erratic policies such as the sudden imposition of the highway liquor ban or the sealing of spaces can play havoc with financials. It is virtually impossible sometimes for an individual restaurateur to bear the financial loss that occurs as a result. Only big players with deep pockets and the means to withstand losses can tide over such unforeseen events.

Saby Gorai, former executive chef at Olive, consultant to several big restaurant projects around the country these days and a man who speaks his mind, spoke to me about the skewed nature of the business of restaurants.

'Comparing hospitals with the hospitality business, hospitals invest 20 per cent of their capital in real estate, restaurants invest 80 per cent. In restaurants, less than 6 per cent of expenditure goes towards paying salaries, in hospitals 37–40 per cent is spent on salaries. Less than 13–14 per cent of hospitals fail, around 87 per cent of restaurants fail,' Saby said. I am not sure where he got these numbers from, or whether these come from his considerable experience setting up restaurants all across the country. But the overall picture these paint is appropriately cautioning even if you take the specific figures with a pinch of salt.

Despite being so heavily dependent on getting the right people, team building and staff training are not given adequate attention, as I see it.

A big part of what makes the business of restaurants tough in India currently is the high cost of real estate. With profit margins being slim, if a newbie restaurateur invests 25–30 per cent of revenue in rent, how will he or she make money? According to conventional wisdom from many restaurateurs and consultant Samir Kukreja, rent must not be more than 15–20 per cent of revenue. However, there are many restaurants that spend far more than this.

Food costs in India have been steadily rising too. Chefs in what is defined as the 'premium casual' segment struggle to keep this food cost to about 30 per cent of revenue. Though, of course, this varies widely depending on the kind of restaurant we are looking at. Fine dining or luxury restaurants like Bukhara or Indian Accent keep food costs at about 25 per cent, according to industry insiders. In general, food cost as a percentage of revenue is less at luxury restaurants because of the higher pricing of the meal. Mid-market restaurants struggle to balance high food costs and lower prices.

Sometimes, ambitious new brands eager to attract attention go overboard with the food budget. I have heard stories of new restaurants running at 70 per cent food cost for the first year because the intention of the restaurateur and chef was to just grab eyeballs. In formats where the price you charge a customer has to be kept low, this is obviously foolhardy.

Sometimes, I hear food critics and rival chefs talk badly of establishments that 'curtail' their food cost. 'How can they have basa on the menu and still claim to be a top-quality restaurant,' is a common jibe. Chef Gaggan Anand of the eponymous Gaggan in Bangkok asked me much the same, claiming that he does not look at the cost of his food at all in Bangkok, that food is his PR and that he manages to sell so much, and so much wine, that his restaurant makes at least a 20 per cent profit.

In India, though, the realities are different. In a long discussion, Anand acknowledged it. With high rents, rising labour costs and people's spending power much lower than in other dining capitals of the world, given that we don't attract many high-paying tourists and consumers don't eat out as frequently as in more mature markets, a restaurant must play the price game, whether it is in the 'luxury' or 'premium' bracket or in the 'casual'. It cannot risk pricing itself out of the market.

If you cannot charge your customers more, obviously you have to make concessions somewhere. As a business, you are forced to cater to diners who want a six-course tasting menu for ₹2,000.

Finding enough talent and then retaining staff are among the biggest challenges restaurateurs report in India. People switch jobs at the drop of a hat and chefs get poached all too easily if a rival restaurateur wants to 'borrow' ideas, dishes and presentations. And rigour in professional cooking and research has been suffering because what the talent crunch and frequent poaching means is that chefs who may be number 2 or 3 in a restaurant's hierarchy often get picked up by a new rival to head their kitchen. This particularly happens in hotels, where hierarchies are strict and promotions slow. Earlier, to progress from a commis chef to executive chef would take a good two decades. While a lot of times, this slow progress could be frustrating, long hours spent in the kitchen by junior chefs meant that there was a certain level of competence and ability to work under high pressure.

The mushrooming of standalones also means that catering college graduates or young chefs who would earlier stick with hotel chains now have more flexibility in changing jobs frequently. Hoteliers often point to chefs with just a year or two of experience who opt out of the hotel hierarchy, refusing to spend long years climbing the ranks or slaving in high-stress kitchens. Instead, they join standalone restaurants, having acquired a Taj or ITC tag after just a year or two of work.

Even at standalones, I have been witness to situations where junior chefs at one restaurant now have the option to head kitchens in another copycat restaurant, essentially replicating the ideas and recipes of their mentors, without the finesse or detail.

For consumers, this means the rampant availability of food where sophistication, nuance and even technical expertise is often sacrificed. Copycat restaurants, in my opinion, have flooded the market with less than adequate cooking standards.

A few fearless but lone voices such as Camellia Panjabi agree. 'Where are chefs these days who spend time researching a cuisine and delving deep into classical Indian recipes?' she asked bluntly as we ate at her casual London restaurant Masala Zone in Covent Garden one afternoon. Though Masala Zone is not a fine-dine, it has nuanced recipes of even something as clichéd as rogan josh. The chillies are smoked, only Kashmiri chillies are used, the rattan jot is from Kashmir to give the colour and all the spices are imported from India. Frankly, I don't think this level of commitment to refined Indian cooking exists in most Indian restaurants today. One reason for that is because chefs no longer have to spend long years training to gain expertise.

Mediocrity in the restaurant space in India passes muster as of now, with just a handful of exceptions. This is also because of the low expectations of diners themselves, as per my observation. A majority of young diners in India today are possibly first- or second-generation frequent restaurant-goers. They may be used to quality food at home, but in restaurants they do not want that sort of homely food. Instead, they want food as entertainment and something 'different', as I have analysed in the first part of the book. Many of these consumers don't really understand or appreciate the difference between a good restaurant and a mediocre one because of a lack of exposure when it comes to food that is not home-cooked or experienced as street eats. This is unlike, say, Italy or Hong Kong, where expectations from even casual restaurants are very high. Mediocrity then is the norm in Indian restaurant-scape because we have a lack of supply in terms of talent and a lack of demand for quality from evolved diners.

For now, if you have eaten even at a modest casual restaurant in many global cities known for their restaurant culture, you will recognize that food quality is high in those cities for the money you pay. At high-end restaurants, the difference is even more remarkable. The Indian customers are more stuck on deals and discounts as a differentiator between restaurants than quality. This is an opinion I have formed after writing on and evaluating restaurants for close to two decades. Are things changing? We will discuss this further in a subsequent chapter.

But first, a major issue which causes many restaurant brands to stumble is scalability. As they aspire to grow, this is a conundrum all restaurants face – how to expand while holding on to quality, service style and everything that made the brand in the first place.

SLIPPING ON SCALE

Arvind Singhal, chairman of Technopak, a retail advisory company, does some quick maths for me one afternoon during a long conversation, pointing to the huge potential for restaurants in India.

With people eating out around four times a month on an average in the top 20 cities in the country, as per Singhal's estimate,[1] any restaurant concept that targets 100 million people in the top 20 cities, and keeps the price of a meal at ₹200–250 (the sweet spot for most mass consumers), Singhal says, will have the potential to do huge business. You can do the maths yourself.

So, why don't we have a ₹1,000–2,000 crore restaurant company, he asks, or anything to match McDonald's (in the QSR space), or Chipotle or Wagamama or Pret a Manger (chains that are fast-casual but offer better-quality product and dining experience than we associate with a typical QSR)? Where is the great Indian high-street restaurant brand?

Many ambitious restaurateurs want to create exactly that, leveraging the natural demographic advantage India offers. However, till now, most restaurateurs have slipped up while pursuing their ambition.

One of the biggest Indian restaurant companies outside of the QSR segment, apart from Barbecue Nation, and the only one operating mixed-format restaurants that is publicly listed, is Speciality Restaurants. The company operates more than 100 restaurants, with popular brands like Mainland China, Oh! Calcutta and Hoppipola, across various segments – from premium casual to bars.

Yet, the company has been on treacherous terrain as far as growth goes. The stress on the company's performance was noted in an *Economic Times* article in December 2018,[2] according to which part of the distress was caused by expansion forced upon it by a private equity investor, which allegedly pushed Speciality to add 50 outlets in just two to three years to grow the company's valuation. Speciality Restaurants did not get patient capital to grow slowly and consolidate its outlets. In addition, there may have been operational problems as well, and perhaps not enough of an audience connect for all the brands – some of which need to be recalibrated to keep up with changing tastes – some industry observers have hypothesized in conversations with me.

In contrast, let us look at a brand like Pret a Manger, the London-headquartered casual-dining chain offering high-quality fresh salads, sandwiches and coffee, which was sold in 2018 for £1.5 billion to investment fund JAB Holdings (owner of Krispy Kreme), according to *Reuters*.[3]

For 10 years before the sale, the 530-outlet global chain had been owned by Bridgepoint Capital, another investment fund that had bought it in 2008 for around £350 million. Over this decade, Pret, as it is popularly called by patrons, rose from being a small local player to a global one, and eventually fetched Bridgepoint six times the money it had invested. What is more, each of the staff got a £1,000 bonus, according to the terms of the sale.

Obviously, what we have before us are two stark examples of growth strategies: One where a PE fund ostensibly pressured a restaurateur to expand rapidly, the other where investors allowed a company to grow gradually. When a restaurateur takes PE money to finance the growth of his brands, it is important to be sure about what kind of money that is – whether it is patient capital or not. Entrepreneurs need to be more cognizant of the challenges presented by trying to go about the intricate and complex business of restaurateuring while having a monkey on their back.

According to a report in the *Financial Times* in June 2019, 'private equity dealmaking has soared to its highest level since the lead up to the global financial crisis, and there is no end in sight to the buyout boom as companies chase investment opportunities for a record amount of unspent cash that totals almost $2.5 tn'.[4] This unprecedented amount of 'dry powder' is ready to buy companies as billions of dollars more are being raised for newer funds.

In the US and the UK, where the PE market is more mature than in India, many funds have been buying entire restaurant companies (instead of partially investing in them while founding restaurateurs operate them, as is mostly the case in India) for a while now and then operating them too, after hiring experts in the field. Some of the best-known restaurant brands in the fast casual segment globally are in fact now owned by private equity funds, including the likes of Pret a Manger, Krispy Kreme, Peet's Coffee, Johnny Rockets, Cinnabon and Popeyes. Private equity in the restaurant space has been on the rise internationally since the mid-2010s, and so it is in India too.

Here, where most PE funds are only partially invested in restaurant companies and may not always have sectoral experts to advise them, restaurant operations are still helmed by the founding restaurateurs. However, as this space matures, PE funds may begin to consider buyout deals or acquiring majority stakes, in which case, if restaurants are a substantial part of their portfolio, they will likely hire experts to operate the companies themselves, says Karan Tanna, a young entrepreneur and CEO of Yellow Tie Hospitality, a restaurant franchisee management company. This is already the case in more mature markets and makes for better business for both the funds and the brands.

Tanna's ambition, he told me, is to build chains. Scale is what he enjoys most and he is interested in mostly taking up pre-existing brands, or new brands entering India, managing them and scaling them up. He genuinely believes that franchising in a systematic and managed way can lead to tremendous growth and that he can create a 1,000-outlet company.

Tanna is just 31, but his own journey with restaurants is interesting. He became a restaurateur in 2012 by taking up a franchise of a small but popular bakery-cum-cafe called Goodies in Ahmedabad. This was a typical mom-and-pop brand and perhaps could not give Tanna the kind of support and standardization that was needed to run a franchise. Tanna shut down his outlet but did not give up on his dream.

By 2014, Tanna was guiding the Gujarati brand Kutchi King, attempting to turn it into a national and even international chain, focused on street foods like dabeli and vada pav. The thought was that if burgers and pizza can make for such huge chains, why can't popular Indian street food dishes? Tanna provided guidance to the brand, developed strict SOPs (standard operating procedures), focused on building marketing strategies and teams and led the brand to grow to about 200 stores, primarily in Gujarat and Maharashtra. The brand exists even now, though Tanna left the business and decided to start Yellow Tie in 2016. His first project was signing up American brand Genuine Broaster Chicken, and in the first year, he grew it to 20–25 stores across India, focusing on menus, a central production facility, recruitment and training of restaurant personnel.

Now, in the space of three years, he has 11 brands under Yellow Tie Hospitality and is looking to grow all these through franchisee management. While some are in the QSR space, others are sit-downs, bars and so on, and he wants to take them all over the country and grow them into large companies.

Karan Tanna then is an interesting person to sit down and have a detailed conversation with on the problems dogging restaurant scalability in India. He is candid and transparent and clear in his thought process about something that he is very passionately interested in.

I agree with Tanna's analysis of the Indian restaurant-scape when he says that the root of the problem lies with most restaurant brands not being designed in a way to be scalable in the first place. 'There are four major things that you need for a brand to be scalable – simply put, it must be a standard product that can be taken all across India, its kitchen processes and front-of-the-house processes must be standardized, the economics of the restaurant should be designed in a pan-India way and not hyperlocal and, finally, the product should be differentiated enough to have a different positioning that attracts a big consumer set,' he points out.

What does all this mean? It is clear to those of us who

analyse Indian restaurants that many of the restaurant companies and brands attempting to scale using PE money in the country currently do not have models which will allow them to go beyond three to four outlets, or sometimes even fewer.

It is obvious that chef-led restaurants have limited scalability. Yet, we see company after company, brand after brand, attempt to scale restaurant concepts that require meticulous and detailed cooking and sourcing, and which have chefs as the face of the brands.

A restaurant like Toast and Tonic in Bengaluru is only one example of this flawed thought process. Dishes created using local seasonal ingredients, involving creativity and precise cooking, work at a single outlet in a city, but this is clearly not a replicable format. As a consumer, for me, there is a clear difference between the second Mumbai outlet and the Bengaluru branch. To take it to a third or fourth outlet will be greatly ill-advised in my opinion.

Apart from processes being standardized, the economics of every branch need to work in the same way whether one is in Mumbai or Raipur for a truly scalable concept. 'McDonald's, for instance, will always buy spaces that are not less than 3,000 sq. ft wherever they are. This is because they need to cater to 300–400 customers on weekends and in the evenings and rely on that scale to make money whether they are in a small town or a big town. Most Indian restaurant brands don't have this,' Tanna says.

There are also differences in customer behaviour and palate. If you have to heavily tweak your restaurant each time you go to a new location, the model is not really suitable for scaling up. Only food that is very simple to prepare like in one-dish restaurants can be replicated consistently at multiple outlets. Similarly, when a restaurateur is creating an 'experience', it is hard to replicate it at multiple outlets because audience tastes are so varied. A chain like Social, one of the few that have worked equally well in almost all the markets they go into, keeps it fresh for newer consumers by making changes to the way the restaurant looks and feels at every location. The food too gets tweaked and menus relevant to individual markets are created. But this is hard work and tricky to achieve. A dedicated team has to constantly watch the brand and keep making adjustments even as it grows rapidly and navigates challenges in every location.

Many restaurant companies also end up opening too many brands and then struggle to manage all these, leading to a loss of management bandwidth. If scaling up is the idea, it may be better to focus on a single brand.

Then there is product differentiation – how your restaurant product (food and experience) stands out from existing competitors. Casual restaurants that have done well as scalable concepts have typically introduced a revolutionary or at least brand-new idea and product into a market where there was a clear gap. McDonald's did that with hamburgers, that was their proprietary product, as Tanna points out, Burger King with 'whoppers' (a different positioning from 'burgers'), Chipotle and Pret a Manger with the premise of freshly cooked food (each Pret, for instance, has a kitchen, though the mis en place comes from a central facility). Basically, your restaurant needs to be positioned in a distinct way.

Look around – how many restaurants do you see offering something really distinct or unique in India? When I examine various markets in Mumbai, Delhi and Bengaluru, all I really see is a sea of concepts offering cafe-ized street food, or cleverly presented pan-Indian food in casual settings, pan-Asian concepts offering sushi, bowls and ramen, Chinese places with dim sum, Cantonese or Schezwan flavours if not Indianized, or just large cafes and bars with a mix of cocktails, a 'global' menu, coffee and the like. Most restaurants have similar menus and not enough to differentiate them from others in the same category. Many rely on cheaper liquor pricing to differentiate themselves from peers and bring in customers (a common pricing strategy in many bars is cheaper priced alcohol and relatively more expensive food), but this is obviously a short-lived game because as others get into the space, they can and do undercut. Discounts and deals seem to be ruling the Indian restaurant market.

These restaurants cannot be scaled up because they are not distinct and will not have an emotional connect with an audience, especially if they hope to leverage adequate numbers and not cater to hyperlocal sensibilities.

If restaurant brands have concepts that are intrinsically not suited to scale and investors try to pressure restaurateurs to grow outlets unrealistically, obviously the bubble will burst, as we can often see from restaurants underperforming or shutting across markets. Even when brands have an inherent scalability in their DNA, PE investors pushing for unrealistic growth is going to ruin the brand. As Tanna says, 'Take a brand like Chaayos [which serves different types of chai and Indian snacky food and is quite scalable], if it is suddenly pushed to grow to, say, 100 stores in two years, obviously, many aspects of what makes a good restaurant – a connect with audiences, understanding them, how the product is served and cooked – will suffer. Once audiences lose interest in a brand, it is very difficult to get them back. It becomes a point of no return.'

Tanna is right. Restaurants are unlike any other businesses. They involve a certain connect with audiences, the ability to craft a unique and engaging experience, which cannot be looked at purely from a mechanistic, numbers point of view. Once customers disengage from a restaurant, it is virtually impossible to bring it back to life. Like Riyaaz Amlani says, 'Scaling in India is a tricky and treacherous business. India is not a homogenous market. A customer's tastes and preferences change considerably; a one-size-fits-all rarely works. Building back-office infrastructure and systems is time-consuming and costly. Negotiating different laws and customs too is slippery. Restaurants are subjected to hyperlocal laws and regulations that vary from state to state, municipal limit to municipal limit sometimes "as the crow flies".'

It is obvious to any observer of the space that while restaurant companies need to carefully evaluate whether they need PE funds at all and who the investors should be, the funds too need a clearer understanding of what models can really be scaled and thus earn money for them, as well as of the operators' unique personalities that impact the business so much.

Much of the problem in India at the moment is also because PE funds investing in the restaurant business do not have much knowledge of restaurateuring and the unique challenges it poses as a business that relies heavily on an emotional connect with its audiences. We can see from the Sagar Ratna example that any attempt to treat it like a general retail business by those who may have experience in retail but not restaurants can backfire badly.

However, as the market is maturing, many of the funds are becoming cognizant of this gap. For instance, L Catterton, the private equity arm of French luxury goods conglomerate LVMH, hired the experienced restaurant CEO Sharad Sachdeva to be director of operations and look after the fund's assets in the GCC countries, Indian and South-east Asia. In India, L Catterton is the majority stakeholder for Riyaaz Amlani's Impresario Entertainment and Hospitality, which runs Social.

With PE funds now becoming aware of how specialized a job restaurateuring is, we will hopefully have a better ecosystem for the growth of restaurant brands.

What restaurateurs on their part need to assess truthfully is whether their concepts are really suited to scaling up. Most restaurants in the premium casual space are only good to go to two or three, perhaps four, locations in the country at most, as per my analysis, not just because they are chef-led, or the experience is niche, requiring unique settings or supplies, but also because the depth of the market in India for upscale restaurant experiences at a higher price points (say, ₹1,000–1,500 per person) is low.

Some markets like Delhi, Mumbai and Bengaluru are deemed to have enough depth in terms of spending power and capacity, population and the culture of eating out, and widely different catchment areas for multiple outlets of the same brand in the same city. However, even so, each restaurateur needs to gauge whether the kind of food or experience they are offering has enough takers in different catchment areas to sustain the business without cannibalizing the sister outlet. An Artusi, the high-quality Italian restaurant, in Gurugram does not have the same resonance with audiences as its original outlet in Delhi's GK II, as per my observation, because it is essentially the same small set of evolved south Delhi/Gurugram diners that form its core customer base. There are perhaps just not enough people to sustain two separate outlets day after day.

In Mumbai, a restaurant outlet in Kamala Mills will obviously eat into the business of its sister outlet in Palladium Mall down the road – it is debatable whether there are enough people to fill two different outlets of the same brand regularly and allow both to make profits. A cafe with outlets in Bandra West and Andheri makes no sense because it is the same people who are divided between both. Like Saransh Goila, chef and restaurateur of takeaway brand Goila Butter Chicken, says, 'I am now in the process of expanding Goila Butter Chicken and have to think about this problem even though I have a smaller delivery format. Ultimately you have to study whether there are enough people to warrant a third or fourth outlet in a city.'

India is unlike any other market in the world because it is more like a continent than a country. Other markets have more homogenous consumers. In India, there are wide chasms between the north and south, east and west, millennial and 'family' audiences, and even between audiences belonging to different subcultures in the same city. Any brand seeking an all-India presence needs to address this, especially if it's doing more complex dishes than simple single-item burgers, ice creams and waffles. Even street food traditions in different parts of the country are diverse and resonate strongly with local audiences. What is accepted by one audience may not find acceptance in another region.

Even a dish like biryani, around which several takeaway and restaurant chains are being built, will be challenging to do at a pan-India level as these chains grow. The traditional dish of connoisseurs, distinguished by the quality of its rice, meat and ghee, has been reduced to a low-brow dish with indistinct recipes for rice and meat bunged in together without necessarily the use of traditional premium ingredients in its mass format. Millennials who need to satiate their hunger, working professionals with no time to cook at home or those who just crave something wholesome and spicy but are not discerning enough are customers of most biryani chains, in my opinion.

However, as many of these new chains multiply outlets and seek to go pan-India, I believe that they will need to be cognizant of cultural connects with the dish and expectations arising out of these. In Kolkata or Hyderabad, for instance, where the local biryani tradition is very strong and individual outlets can be spotted in every marketplace, will there be enough patrons for biryani chains? Similarly, in Chennai or Lucknow, where again local traditions for specific kinds of biryani are very strong and there are already local chains or local mom-and-pop favourites who supply the dish, will a pan-India chain find a foothold? It will be interesting to watch the dynamics.

In other large cities, where the migrant workforce is large or where millennials have not had the opportunity to taste a well-made, region-specific biryani, chains may do well because they have a product that is hugely popular but not really freely available.

Saransh Goila's Goila Butter Chicken in Mumbai is essentially a takeaway and not an experience-led restaurant, but it has immense scope for scaling up, in my opinion. Like biryani or vada pav, here is a dish that large sections of the population crave. Thanks to the globalization of the palate and the building of a common youth culture based on similar taste in films, music and politics, butter chicken is no longer a Delhi or Punjabi phenomenon. It is a dish widely known and one that people have nostalgia for but not necessarily available easily outside Delhi. Saransh's butter chicken is a proprietary product – his sauce stands out from the usual recipes (he smokes it) and his social media and TV presence means that the product is now linked to him in the minds of many of his millennial followers. He already has four outlets in Mumbai at the time of writing, and the chain has immense potential in my opinion to go pan-India, provided he finds mature and patient investors who give him time to stabilize the product in each region.

Smartly, Saransh did not start Goila Butter Chicken in Delhi at all – despite it being his home city. Had he done so, his butter chicken would have immediately encountered a huge wall of resistance from consumers who have specific small restaurants they patronize for the dish. In Mumbai, the field was open, and if he goes to Bengaluru, he will likely find success there too. In cities that are culturally more closed and insular than these metros, converting local palates used to very different tastes may be a problem. However, with the internet, things have changed dramatically as far as pop culture trends go. Unlike people of even a generation ago, consumers today are much more open to new ideas. In many ways, cultural diversity is dying – which is not a great thing. However, for restaurateurs trying to scale up, it has its benefits.

Another way around for chains wanting to scale up can be to look at relatively unfamiliar foreign foods that have a resonance with the Indian palate. The success of small waffle stalls in many metros is a case study – how this dish that most Indians who have never been to Belgium and never tasted in its original form has found so much acceptance in middle-class India.

Because there is no history of waffles in any part of the country and because the taste is so general (sweet), there is no prejudice against the dish. Instead, because the taste of sugar is well loved and compound chocolate is what most Indians recognize as chocolate, waffles topped with synthetic chocolate sauce offer a very sellable mix of a new idea with familiar flavours.

In Mumbai, Bayroute, a chain of upscale Middle Eastern food, has been offering great quality food with a lively vibe. There are several outlets throughout the city, and to my mind, it would do fantastically well in other cities too because here is a cuisine that many middle-class Indians can understand, yet aspire to and that really is not so easily available barring the mandatory mezze platters at almost every casual restaurant. Bayroute's offerings are imaginative, fun and detailed and it could be a great hit with consumers in many different parts of the country.

The thing to worry about when such a chain tries to grow is how consistent the product offering will remain. What makes Bayroute click is the higher than usual quality of food, its cheerful, casual service, and the vibe of its spacious sit-downs. All of these need to remain consistent at every location.

Restaurants where the entire experience is the key rather than just a single proprietary product are harder to scale up for obvious reasons – consistency, supply chains, management, high costs and a lack of talent. Restaurants that are chef-led and even more complicated in the food and service experience they are offering or that are catering to niche sensibilities that cannot get a large enough audience must not try to scale up if they want to retain their brands.

Danny Meyer, the New York-based restaurateur and CEO of Union Square Hospitality, is one of the most influential restaurateurs in the world. But he confesses to a fear of scaling up. In an interview to *Forbes* magazine,[5] Meyer, who has always considered himself to be a creator and operator of 'small businesses', linked his fear of scalability to his fear of going bankrupt – something that had happened to his father when he tried to grow his travel business.

Meyer has founded some of the most successful and respected restaurants, cafes and bars in New York. Apart from the upscale and niche restaurants he created, he famously founded the behemoth Shake Shack in 2004, after getting fascinated by the idea of a hot dog stall. After the first one, it took Meyer five years to open the second, because he feared expanding. The idea, though, was simple: to sell high-quality food but keep it limited to just burgers and shakes, products that can be cooked or assembled easily and consistently at multiple locations. The idea was perfect for expansion. However, Meyer took it slowly and only took Shake Shack public a full decade later. The brand continues to pull in about $445 million in annual revenues from 200 outlets.

The biggest takeaway, though, is that Meyer left the running of Shake Shack to CEO Randy Garutti, a long-time Union Square Hospitality employee, and went back to creating the single restaurants he loves. 'I'm happy to dance with giants,' he said in the interview, 'but I'm not one.'

Many Indian restaurateurs need to realize what their heart really tells them. Do they want to create relatively small, single restaurants or do they want to create a big chain that will pull in large crowds? The sensibilities of both these businesses are completely different, and to be good at either, you have to be a certain kind of person. 'Scale involves a completely different mindset,' says Sameer Seth, co-founder of The Bombay Canteen, who once worked at Tabla, owned by Meyer's Union Square Hospitality. A mind that enjoys the creativity of setting up a restaurant with many individualistic touches, detailed and high-quality or innovative food, and who wants to constantly engage with their audience, is a niche player. The mind that enjoys serving vast numbers and has personal tastes and sensibilities that put them in touch with a mass audience is completely different.

Indian chefs and restaurateurs need to introspect on who they are and what they truly desire – acclaim, recognition and, well, the ego boost that comes with spotlighting creativity and treading new ground? Or creating a large company where the founder may well be anonymous? I feel most Indian restaurateurs and chefs are confused. You cannot grow a McDonald's, or an Indian Pret, or a Kebab Factory, and be recognized for the glamour of your cooking and restaurateuring.

Interview with Sharad Sachdeva, director of operations, L Catterton Asia

- **Are PE funds still bullish about the restaurant business (not food tech) in India?**

  PE funds are bullish for anything which has a real return on investment. In the restaurant business, there aren't many success stories, and many companies have poor unit economics or sit on a negative EBITDA on store levels. The story becomes grimmer if you add corporate cost to these reeling losses.

  To specifically answer you, there aren't many sizeable/profitable restaurant chains which can attract the fancy of decent-sized funds; however, there have been small strategic investments here and there. It's a mixed response from the PE the fraternity towards the restaurant business.

- **We often hear about PE funds pressuring operators to grow more and more outlets, unviably, leading to the**

eventual collapse of a brand. In your opinion, is there a larger picture to this?

There could be cases where the promoter faces pressure from the PE. However, many companies are run as mom/pop/lala shops; when an investor comes in, he first tries to change the mindset of the top management and then starts to put in processes. I am sure you know this analogy that most times people exert so much energy to resist the change that if they put in half of it, they can adapt to the change. That fantastically applies here.

There definitely is a pressure to multiply because that is the basic premise of the so-called marriage between a company and a PE fund; when the fund invests, there is a decided path of expansion which the promoter needs to deliver in a certain specific time, and when a fund doesn't see that happening, there has to be certain logical pressure. The degree of pressure can vary from fund to fund, and the perception of that degree differs in understanding from promoter to promoter. There have been cases where funds exerted pressure for expansion and promoters without much thought or due diligence just signed sites, only to bleed later – the wrong strategy by any standard. But whose fault is it? A promoter can say the fund bullied and the fund can say the promoter didn't deliver.

The best strategy would be to sit across a table and decide the roll-out plan and do mindful expansion. Like how we at L Catterton do. Mutual trust plays an important part in such matters. The brand can die if random expansion is done and can multiply its evaluation several times if done in a mindful and decided way. If the brand springs to success, both parties are responsible and vice versa.

- **What are the problems funds face with family-/promoter-led businesses? Internationally, funds now**

majorly invest in restaurants and hire hospitality professionals to advise and run the businesses themselves. Is that a possibility in India?

In family-run businesses, the main problems are complex shareholding, a lackadaisical approach, less dependency on tech, approvals on face value, lack of due diligence in critical matters, etc. The complexity increases multi-fold if the business is in second generation. A good fund mostly clears these hurdles during the due diligence process and starts the relationship with a relatively clearer slate. In case there are still some legacy issues and dinosaurical processes, then those are also anticipated by most professional funds and weaved into the contract by way of allowing them to hire a professional team at the CXO level and wade through issues in the post-acquisition period.

In family-/promoter-run businesses, if an individual's ego is bigger than process or procedure, thereby giving a back seat to approval systems and delegation of power, in such a situation a professional investment team from the fund's side realizes this during the course of negotiations and builds the contract in such a way that they get realistic powers to introduce systems and make everyone realize that processes would be systems-driven rather than individual-driven.

In most cases, personal rapport with the promoter plays a vital role. It is my personal experience that you have to win over the promoter with your good work and convince him that you are in his system to add value and make his life easier. Never thrust yourself, find a subtle way!

- **Are most casual dining brands or bars in India really scalable? Is there a problem with many models?**

Yes, casual dining bars are really scalable, though the scalability depends on zillions of factors. What I have realized is that consumers want to visit new, quirky concepts, so the same concept has to reinvent itself through innovation every few years if not months!

Yes, there are chef-led, organic-food- or local-produce-centric concepts and they have investments from different funds. Sometimes the promoter is so convincing and passionate about a very quirky concept that he convinces the fund about the scalability, which at times is not the case when the rubber hits the road. Sometimes, fund managers get carried away with the passion the promoter exudes and buy a stake in a very niche concept thinking it to be a scalable model, but reality isn't always the same.

Every fund has a different mantra; some are dormant partners (just investors), some are active partners (want to know everything but they don't know ground realities, mostly boardroom discussion to decide what's to be done or not). Very few engage themselves in every aspect of the business. At L Catterton, we engage in every aspect of the business, be it business development for new sites, operations with same-store sales growth, key hires, marketing, etc. We discuss in the boardroom and roll up our sleeves to execute it on ground. To me this is the secret sauce behind the success of companies and funds in the long run.

6

SPICING IT UP: PUBLICITY, PR AND SOCIAL MEDIA

Instagram has changed the world – especially the food world. Zizzi, a chain of Italian restaurants in the UK, researched the habits of millennials, according to the *Independent*,[1] and found that 18- to 35-year-olds spend five whole days a year browsing food images on Instagram, and as many as 30 per cent of consumers would avoid a restaurant if its Instagram presence was weak.

I am not sure how much of that is true and how much of that happens in India. Bloggers, 'influencers' and those engaged in the digital space certainly seem to believe that their posts matter and that people get influenced enough to go visit a restaurant at least once. From my own observations, it often happens that when a new restaurant opens, scores of 'influencers' get invited to party there. Some of these influencers or food groups are even invited to host tables; some of them charge the restaurant to host these tables. Grand events are planned to launch restaurants, chefs, new menus. The idea in general is to generate 'buzz', with big marketing spends aiding it.

Cut to six months down the line. Or even three. A new place generates similar buzz. Consumer attention rapidly shifts. The older place begins to show signs of strain. The bubble is burst and there is a struggle to find actual paying customers. If the investors have deep pockets, they invest more in another round of publicity. A food award or two may be bagged through cronies, networks or just by plainly buying these (these are open secrets in the industry; I wrote about the hollowness of food awards in India in an article for *The Hindu*).[2] But actual diners per se seem to be unmoved by all these awards. This cycle of artificially manufactured publicity may continue for one or two or even three years. But the restaurant eventually shuts, or changes its name and concept to emerge as a new one if there is something intrinsically wrong with the product or the market it is pitched to.

Instagram and social media can help a restaurant or an idea reach many people at a much lower cost than conventional advertising. However, this sort of a buzz cannot make a long-lasting brand. Restaurateurs who are in the business for the long haul and not just as a short-term gig need to realize this basic truth. No publicity or PR can help a product that is fundamentally flawed. Egos can pull it on for a while, even years (if the pockets are particularly deep or if it is a vanity project) but it will not be a viable business and it will not really have brand recall and pull.

There seems to be a crisis of credibility when it comes to the food media in India at the moment, and while this is worse in the space of online food influencers, it is also true within traditional media. In many mature markets, like London or New York, influential food critics writing for newspapers are taken seriously by customers. Their ratings matter and restaurant businesses are affected as a result of their reviews. In India, very few critics and writers have that stature and credibility. By and large, food media in the country seems to have surrendered to marketing managers and is reduced to being part of the PR machinery for restaurants that no one takes seriously.

My belief that any PR machinery and the influencers it seeks to cultivate ultimately cannot make or break any restaurant is borne out by the failure or lacklustre performance of many restaurants that no one remembers even a year after the launch party. I don't want to point fingers here, but the examples abound. In fact, this is not a uniquely Indian condition. Despite what the Zizzi survey may have found, restaurants have shut regardless of considerable investment in marketing and PR – because when there are operational issues, when restaurateurs do not know their market or their business in and out, when investors have problems between themselves, when the quality of a product does not match what the customer expects, then no amount of PR and marketing can help. Talli Joe in London – which opened with great fanfare in 2016 as a modern Indian bar-centric restaurant kind of modelled on The Bombay Canteen – shut down after roughly two years because of a series of problems; this, despite the fact that when it had opened, it had managed to get quite a lot of PR-led publicity.

As its former head chef Sameer Taneja told me, in her view, the reasons were: Positioning was unclear; whether it was a bar-led restaurant or a restaurant, it didn't make commercial sense as rent and rates were too high. Consistency was an issue (after Sameer left, his position was not filled for a year). Owners were involved in daily operations but did not have operational experience.

However, where PR and marketing helps is when the operations are solid; then, it has the potential to increase the brand's influence, as we can also see from international examples of undiscovered gastronomic regions such as Peru and top restaurants that were 'discovered' thanks to marketing activities by tourism boards and perception marketing by restaurants themselves.

There are some restaurateurs who do not believe in PR and marketing though, believing that word of mouth is the best form of advertising. Have they been less successful? How are their restaurants doing? It would be interesting to pause and take note of their business.

Word-of-mouth publicity is of great importance to

restaurants because it involves trust. People are influenced by somebody whose judgement they know they can rely on, in choice of both restaurant and dishes to order. In fact, even globally, brands and Instagram are beginning to acknowledge the role of 'micro influencers' who are perceived to be more credible in their domains because they have expertise and credibility, rather than the large body of 'professional influencers' exposed to be working as marketing machines. (It is strange that many of these individuals, who hold no other jobs, introduce themselves as 'influencers', when asked what is it they do. An influencer is certainly not an influencer if that is the job description!)

A micro influencer can be anyone. Your neighbour, friend, relative or an expert whose word you trust and who may not even know how they are influencing your choice. They first get the word out, which gets gradually amplified as more and more people go and verify for themselves the truth of the micro influencer's claim. This is how word of mouth has functioned for who knows how long. One recent restaurant that started off running, instead of crawling, from its first day because it was able to organically leverage such word-of-mouth publicity in the age of Instagram is Kappa Chakka Kandhari in Chennai.

Chef and restaurateur Regi Mathew, who owns the brand along with two friends, wanted the brand to have a resonance with the Malayali community. This was in sync with the deep research he had done, bringing recipes from small towns, villages and families to a commercial restaurant format. If people from Kerala recognized the restaurant, it would validate that research too, obviously.

For two years, as he was doing the research, Mathew and his partners held a few pop-ups in Bengaluru and even in Dubai, which have substantial Malayali populations. Hundreds of people were made to try the food, their reactions sought. This resulted in an organic social media community for Mathew and his food. When Kappa Chakka Kandhari opened in Chennai, Mathew who had planned an entire media campaign, found that he did not have to spend anything on publicity. There were people, mostly from Kerala, but others too, flocking in from the first day itself! 'People who had liked the food told their friends and relatives in Chennai that we are opening a restaurant and to go try whatever their favourite dish was from the pop-ups,' he points out.

Marut Sikka, another restaurateur, never courts obvious publicity for any of his restaurant launches. There may be a few parties for friends and acquaintances, and Sikka is definitely well connected with the movers and shakers of fashion, arts and lifestyle. However, we never see big bashes or social media or even mainstream media publicity accompanying any of his restaurants. In fact, he has to be one of the quietest restaurateurs around, not visible publicly since his short TV stint a few years ago.

Sikka's Delhi Club House is one of the most successful Indian restaurants in the NCR, consistently packing in large numbers at its outlets both in RK Puram and in Gurugram, even when neighbouring restaurants at the same venues are not doing well.

The outlets do good business according to every industry insider I have spoken to, yet I have never seen anything written about Delhi Club House's shami kebab, or its idli with ghee from Madurai, or its cocktails, by the usual food media.

However, the restaurant is warmly recommended by all sorts of people, including my diplomat friends with no idea about Indian restaurants who suggest it to newcomers in their social circle. It is one of the few that have done financially well in the Sangam complex in Delhi's RK Puram, otherwise the graveyard for high-profile, publicity-courting restaurants. Brands like The Fatty Bao (now shut) serving modern Asian food, and Nueva serving South American food in the same mall, for instance, did not attract even a fraction of the audience that Delhi Club House did, despite the humungous amount of initial buzz that accompanied the launch of these restaurants. Delhi Club House is a great example of how effective word-of-mouth publicity can be for restaurants, if the product is solid and consistent.

A restaurant whose strength lies in its food is best served by slow, organic publicity, I believe. Bars or restaurants dependent on faddish concepts, performances and so on do seek buzz, but this is short-lived and, in my opinion, the return on investment for the kind of marketing money spent is fairly low.

Slow and consistent publicity if carried out with conviction for a brand that has some innate value and is qualitatively different from its competition can pay big dividends. If you track the evolution of Noma, you will see what I mean. In 2003, Rene Redzepi and Claus Meyer opened the restaurant in Copenhagen in an old warehouse; the next year, they organized a Nordic Cuisine Symposium, calling on about a dozen Scandinavian chefs to draft and sign a manifesto on the 'new Nordic kitchen'. Early publicity started emerging thereafter, pointing to the new kind of food they were creating and how the simplest of ingredients was exalted in their kitchen. A Michelin star followed in 2005, and by 2006, the international media had begun to pay notice to the three-year-old restaurant. Noma got reviewed by the *Guardian* at this time and found its first mention in the *Times*.[3] In 2008, when Redzepi and Meyer set up an experimental kitchen on a houseboat, the restaurant was praised in the *Times*, which started the talk about it heralding a new kind of Nordic gastronomy. This was five years after it had opened. By this time, Noma was also in the top 10 on the San Pellegrino list of the world's 50 Best Restaurants. In 2010, seven years after its debut in Copenhagen, Noma became number one on this influential list; global gastronomic tourists came seeking it and others of its kind in Denmark – the creation of a slow and steady global influence.

In India, restaurants seeking buzz in their first years may arrive with a bang but shut with a whimper, in the absence of strong fundamentals. Any new restaurateur must make sure that they are not carried away by the glamour of launch parties.

If budgets are tight, it is better to put money into operations rather than publicity. Also, when getting online influencers, one thing to remember is that the number of views or hits does not necessarily translate into sales. An influencer is an influencer only when they are credible and relevant to your audience.

THE BUSINESS OF BARS

One of the biggest changes in the past five years has been how alcohol has become a common part of social interaction among India's urban youth. Unlike even a decade ago, today, it is common for women to meet each other over wine or cocktails. Dates are conducted over drinks and not necessarily coffee or McDonald's burgers. Office-goers bond over beer after work and dinners are usually accompanied by drinks. India's bar culture has been on an upswing as a response to this change in urban lifestyle – not just in the metros but also in smaller towns like Lucknow, Kanpur, Pune, Nagpur, Vizag, Jaipur et al. In all these towns, we have been seeing chic, upscale bars come up as spaces for younger people to meet, greet and eat. These are unlike the less-inclusive spaces of yesteryears (which, of course, still abide) which were primarily men-only zones, seen as places for cheap alcohol to get drunk on.

Because of this boom, anyone entering the restaurant space comes with the perception that bars make more money faster than food-led concepts (where the food sales account for more than 50 per cent of the total). Indeed, if you look at the restaurant-scape in Delhi, Gurugram, Mumbai, Bengaluru and even Pune, Hyderabad and so on, you will immediately see the predominance of bars in the standalone segment. Old-style family restaurants are falling into oblivion and it seems that everyone is opening a gastropub, or bars with lots of food, whether it is modern Indian, Chinese or pan-Asian, or mixed global bites.

These hybrid concepts are ruled by their bars – during the day, they may function as restaurants, cafes or co-working spaces, but in the evenings and certainly on weekends, you see them become bars with loud music and more liquor sales than food sales.

On the face of it, bars do make more money and quicker money than food-centric restaurants.

A restaurateur in Gurugram, who asked not to be named, in a private conversation with me compared his monthly revenue of ₹2 crore to that of a food-driven restaurant next to his premises, where the space is half (thus, so is the rent) but sales are only one-fourth (₹50 lakh).

However, in the past two years, there has been a growing discussion around the different bar formats in India and what actually works – beyond the hype. For a while, big 5,000 sq. ft spaces selling 80 per cent alcohol and 20 per cent food, relying on mass customers or young customers who primarily came on weekends to party over cheap drinks and all-you-can-drink-and-eat deals, seemed to be working. These were places that made a lot of money on weekends even if they ran half empty during most weekdays.

In fact, anecdotally, many industry insiders say many of these bars seemed to have made so much money on weekends alone that they were able to pay off their capital investment well within one year itself (according to insiders, some did this in as little as six months), and were operationally breaking even from day one. They were able to do this because young customers were driven in through social media buzz around a new offering as well as the lure of all-inclusive deals and cheaply priced alcohol.

When some of these places shut after a year or two, or changed names and themes and lingered on, or just lingered on with much fewer customers post the initial golden run, investors had already recovered their money and the core team that had set up these had already moved on to set up another bar somewhere. Whether the brand lived or died did not matter to many.

These kinds of formats will continue to exist – provided restaurateurs are able to pull in investors lured by the glamour of nightlife and customers seeking buzz and cheaper drinks. However, lately, many restaurateurs who had cracked this format are now looking at mixed-format 'bar-restaurants' that play up a higher quality of food almost as much as drinks and aspire to a 60:40 ratio of alcohol and food sales. Why are bar-preneurs looking to up their food game and focus as much on the bites they offer as on the drinks?

One of the things about running any bar that is centred on 'buzz' and cheap alcohol is that longevity becomes problematic. The party crowd comes in when the bar is new but gravitates to the next new one in just a few months. Then, if cheap alcohol is the only differentiator, another new restaurant can come along and undercut the existing bar or dole out the same kind of drinks in a new setting. It is more difficult to lose customers this fast if food is a differentiator, since food is tougher to copy, especially if it is of a reasonable quality or unique.

This is not to say that food does not get copied. Zorawar Kalra's Farzi Café may have kick-started the trend of modern Indian street food accompanied by high-energy bars, but then there was a spate of bar spaces copying this format ad nauseam. Quirky presentations, foams and airs were deployed by all and sundry for theatrics and without thought.

Still, this kind of copying took time, which is why long after Farzi started the trend (it has evolved ever since, particularly in locations such as Delhi and London), we can still see it in bits and pieces in smaller towns and copycat bars.

Today, while there may be a smattering of these me-too bars relying on a refashioning of popular street flavours, the audience in the metros seems bored of the theatrics, and we're finally seeing molecular's last sighs. Bar owners are thus changing their menus to give us upgraded Indian dishes and drinks sans the smoke and airs.

Similarly, micro-breweries with their focus on many different flavoured lagers (which tasted uniformly sweet, mild and sans distinction; a taste profile many of us dub 'nimbu paani') and bites such as mezze platters and 'overloaded' nachos trended for a while wherever they were allowed legally.

Then there are mixed restaurant-bar-workspace-retail formats that want their spaces to earn them money through the day, every day of the week, and want to attract diverse customers for diverse purposes. Given the high rents in the metros, this seems like a sensible strategy for any large restaurant or bar. Customers frequenting the bar between 8 p.m. and midnight on weekends may not be enough to generate business in the long run.

However, the thing with all these concepts where the bar is central is that they need to change frequently. Social, a pioneer of the co-working concept (but where the bar is equally important), is a successful concept because every outlet changes and refurbishes every two years or so to keep pace with the changing tastes and culture of the young audience it attracts.

If cheap liquor is the only differentiator (instead of the food or entertainment or experience), bar longevity suffers because once the audience is bored, or once someone else comes along offering similar or cheaper prices, the audience vanishes.

However, any large-format bar by definition must play in the mass segment – where lower prices are what drive in customers. This is because India lacks a relatively large base of 'sophisticated', higher-spending consumers or tourists. Average per person spends are the highest in pubs and bars among all other casual restaurant concepts (₹700–1,500, according to the NRAI 2019 report); however, to fill in a 150-cover bar day in and day out, and to justify the rent of a premium space, bar owners have to play the value game.

This means that high-quality cocktails or food that must charge a premium are often not viable in these large spaces. If your dream is to open a really high-quality bar with exclusive cocktails instead of the main business coming from cheaper ones, straight drinks or shots, a smaller 60-seater even in an offbeat location may work. You can see this in the example of the much-loved, very low-key Cocktails and Dreams Speakeasy, a bar in Gurugram owned by mixologist Yangdup Lama. It is surprising that the bar never makes it to any nightlife awards – perhaps a commentary on the credibility of many of these awards. But it is one of the finest in India. These kind of bars are also tough to run because their quality implies a very high level of personal involvement by the face of the brand.

Big formats may make for high top lines, but often only because they play the discount game, while paying high rents. A small bar in an offbeat location may make reasonable profit. Unfortunately, however, many state laws in India (every state has its own licensing policy) do not differentiate in the licensing costs for big and small bars, making it unviable for smaller operations.

This is why India does not have the kind of niche, sophisticated small bars that are the norm all over the world. All these are factors that you have to consider when you decide to set up a bar; and the way to begin is obviously by asking yourself the question, what attracts you to a bar? Great cocktails? The prospect of making quick money? Or the glamour of parties?

Currently, one of the most in-demand formats for bars in India that all restaurateurs with money and ambition want to build is the 'Zuma', 'Sexy Fish' or 'Hakkasan' format. Essentially, these are large glamorous mixed-format spaces with expensive drinks and quality food that can transform themselves equally into a dining destination or a drinking destination for an older (aged 30–50), more sophisticated crowd. These sort of restaurants-with-bars have done well in cities like Dubai and London (with the tourist crowd mostly).

Since in India consumers like to eat with their drinks – we do not have the culture of aperitivo like in southern Europe, or of going out for drinks after dinner at bars which offer only alcohol and scant food – and since an older crowd is more likely to be able to pay a premium on quality experiences, these kinds of formats theoretically seem likely to work.

However, the most obvious challenge in most markets in India remains that of filling up huge bar spaces with enough people willing to spend enough money on higher quality of food, drink and sophisticated experience.

This is not easy to do because India has a much smaller percentage of high-paying customers than markets like London, Dubai or even Bangkok, which see more sophisticated consumers as well as a much higher tourist inflow. The other challenge is the problem of quality creations by chefs and bartenders themselves. This is something that is not talked about enough, but it is a fact that very few chefs and bartenders in India offer originality and top-class creativity. Most restaurants and bars, regardless of the price they command, tend to be derivative, without innovation and of middling quality. I say this from personal observation and experience. This difference in creativity and quality consciousness is stark when you travel and see bars and restaurants in gourmet regions from Melbourne to Hong Kong, Singapore to San Francisco, San Sebastian to New York. In India, at the moment, in most cases, neither does the customer demand quality nor does the chef or mixologist provide it. Perhaps this is going to change in the next few years.

WHAT DO CUSTOMERS WANT?

Over the course of my many informal interactions with chefs and restaurateurs, I have often heard one complaint in particular – Indian consumers do not want or appreciate high-quality food or drinks. They seem happy with pocket-friendly mediocrity. Let us examine this notion.

From my observations, there may be some truth to the perception that we are less demanding as customers when it comes to quality food than those in more developed restaurant markets around the world. Look at the average restaurant meal that you get in India at whatever price point. Now, compare this to average meals in cities such as New York, London, Melbourne and even Singapore and Hong Kong. If you compare like with like and allow for parity of purchasing power, you may agree with me when I say that the quality of food is higher in most of these cities in terms of ingredients used and skilfulness of cooking.

We are not talking about whether you get better and more authentic Italian or French or Japanese food internationally than in India or whether you have a wider range of international cuisines in melting pots like New York or London. After all, Italian food in Italy cannot compare to what passes off as Italian in many parts of the world, and certainly not in India. And a culture of diversity of cuisines within restaurants is only possible when a city has a huge mixed population of expats, travellers and migrants, which Delhi and even Mumbai, the biggest and more diverse restaurant markets in the country, do not.

For that matter, Indian food in most parts of the world cannot be of the same quality that we get in India. That has got to do with availability of ingredients and audience tastes – any audience not exposed to global flavours will expect tastes to be tailored to their palates. Even in London, the most advanced market by far for Indian food, the chicken tikka masala stereotype still exists outside of the expensive, upscale Indian diners because that is all the mass customers who have never been to India have been exposed to. (Though the last is now changing as more people become aware of regional Indian food.)

Similarly, Indian mass audiences are not exposed to many international foods. They like the idea of eating these – but suitably tailored to their tastes. There are many examples of this from the way waffles are done in India to pink pasta, tandoori momos, baos with fried stuff dunked in mayo so that it becomes chaat-like and so on.

What is astonishing, however, is that in general Indian audiences do not even seem to appreciate quality Indian food. If you take a look around, you will see most Indian restaurants in the mid-market space doing versions of modern Indian – essentially where street food is being poshed up in various ways, combined with other tastes from another part of the country, and served with big bold flavours. This is the kind of food that younger Indian diners seem to like – delicious to their palates already used to hot, crunchy, sweet-sour-chilli mishmash.

We don't really have fine restaurants serving more refined classical Indian food – dishes created for the erstwhile royals or aristocrats or trading and knowledge communities known to be gourmet that exemplified the height of culinary creativity of that day by skilful chefs who were better trained, paid and esteemed than the bazaar cooks. Barring a select few, we don't have chefs truly researching quality dishes from homes in different parts of the country, traditions where spicing is specific and restrained and where high-quality ingredients are used, in contrast to most restaurant cooking.

In short, restaurants serve low-brow restaurantized food in general and Indian audiences seek this kind of food while eating out rather than better prepared food, which is more nuanced and more 'authentic' to specific traditions. Restaurants that try to build a lot of rigour in their cooking often complain that not many are willing to pay a premium for this quality. In contrast, average food that can be presented in unusual, even gimmicky ways seems to be better accepted.

This consumer behaviour is in stark contrast to the behaviour of many consumers internationally – in Hong Kong, Tokyo, Rome, Paris, et al., where customers want traditional high-quality food even within restaurants, and demand quality by way of good ingredients and precise cooking even when they are at lower-priced restaurants. It is my hypothesis that, in India, restaurant audiences seem to not insist on quality in the same way because the kind of food that we have eaten at home traditionally has always been different from the kind of food we have eaten 'outside'.

If you go back and read the first couple of chapters, tracing the history and evolution of restaurants and eating out in India, you would come to the same realization. Indians, even when not very well off, are careful and relatively discerning about food at home.

However, since traditionally people have always eaten bolder, more overpowering flavours at restaurants, that's what they flock to, rather than seeking high-quality ingredients but restrained cooking. This ingrained behaviour pattern seems to dog us till now. It is slowly changing, and we can see the huge interest in regional cuisines 'authenticated' by home cooks at pop-ups and food festivals. That may be because traditional

Indian cuisines are disappearing even from homes, given an increasing globalization of the Indian palate.

You only have to examine the tiffin boxes of middle-class children in schools to know that home-made pasta, burgers, wraps and quinoa salads, and fried frozen titbits, have replaced traditional cooking in general. When a generation grows up on this, it may see regional, traditional Indian foods as 'exotic' and restaurants may see acceptance for this kind of food go up.

In India, luxury or upscale restaurants that can command a premium for the ingredients and the chef's superior cooking are also very few. Restaurants like The Table and Indian Accent often complain how rich Indians are ready to drop $300–400 on meals abroad but don't want to spend that kind of money within India.

The idea that luxury dining is more than the sum of the ingredients that a restaurant is serving you is still hard to accept for many Indians, even in the highest social strata – people who expect top service, ambience and experience but seem reluctant to pay for all this. An actor complaining of being 'overcharged' for two bananas in a five-star hotel, expecting to pay the same price as they would at a street vendor's stall (an incident that took social media by storm) encapsulates this mindset.[1]

The Table's Gauri Devidayal pointed out to me that it took years for her restaurant to get customer loyalty and how people even now at her highly regarded restaurant sometimes fail to understand why the cost of a salad should be ₹600. 'In a high-end restaurant, you are paying for many more things than just food – the quality of staff and service, ambience, wine and menus are structured taking all that into account. Yet people don't quite understand that,' she said.

For standalone restaurants, the ability to command higher prices for quality is also impacted by another perception governed by the history of restaurateuring in India, where exclusive restaurants were only within five-star hotels, which connoted prestige. Most of India's best restaurants today are not within hotels but are standalones. But even after almost two decades of the standalone revolution, customers seem to be stuck in the mindset that if it is an independent restaurant, it cannot be as expensive as a 'five-star'.

Hotel-restaurants can command higher prices even if they serve pizza because Indian customers still think of them as truly fine dining. A fine-dine standalone, meanwhile, must peg itself lower, as chef Manish Mehrotra told me during one conversation. 'Our prices have to be always less than a five-star's regardless of the calibre of the restaurant.' (A non-vegetarian tasting menu at Indian Accent costs ₹3,900 plus taxes at the time of writing.)

What many people miss is that the term 'fine dining' connotes a formal restaurant – white table-clothed in the French/European context, meals served ceremoniously, or in courses, usually accompanied by high-quality wine; a restaurant where you are conscious of the ceremony and pomp, where there is a dress code and more. Expensive dining is not necessarily fine dining. Most restaurants within hotels in India are in fact only more expensive than the standalones and not actually fine dining.

Fine dining the world over attracts very few customers and is seen as being on the wane in an age where people are more inclined towards ease and informality, where the very idea of luxury is changing. In India, millennials, the largest spenders, obviously are not attracted to fine-dines – even a formal restaurant like Dum Pukht at ITC Maurya with all its Lucknowi *nazakat* and ceremony has its own older clientele.

Ironically, even hotels these days don't want to invest in fine-dining restaurants because of the low returns on investment. I spoke to Jasjit Singh Assi, who was a star hotel manager at Four Seasons Mumbai till some time ago, and revolutionized the food and beverage set-up there through pop-up experiences that the hotel partnered with, creating an image for itself as a gourmet destination. What Assi told me is interesting: the average millennial is comfortable only in casual, mid-priced settings and fancier restaurants are 'occasion-driven'. 'While it would take ₹7–10 crore to set up a luxury/fine-dine restaurant, a premium casual one can be done in ₹3–4 crore,' he said, and this would offer better returns on investment. Hotel restaurants today want to play in the mid-priced segment too, serving 'comfortable' food that will not necessarily challenge the diner and take them out of their comfort zone. That kind of food has a very limited audience in India, where exposure to international cuisines is low, where people have been used to eating quality food at home but not the same type of food within restaurants, and where, above all, people do not have the capacity to pay the high prices that such quality often demands.

This does not mean that no one should attempt to raise the level of restaurant dining in the country. Fine dining – as defined by its formal service style, high-end ingredients and superlative, exceptional cooking – may be a tough format to attempt because of a smaller audience pool with the appropriate spending capacity and a tendency to treat food with a certain reverence, and because we do not have enough high-end tourists or international travellers who can fill up too many of these restaurants. However, there is an audience for every kind of food in the country, you just have to speak to it.

Many expensive restaurants overprice themselves because they are simply deluded that they are fine dining, when in fact they are not sufficiently differentiated on quality from many others similar to them in the mid-market space.

It is commonly believed that the Indian customer is value conscious and therefore fine dining does not work in India. This needs to be examined carefully and corrected. Value and price are not the same thing, as most people assume. Value is a measure of perception, unlike price. An expensive meal may still offer enough value to a consumer if it is qualitatively high or unique. It is my belief that the Indian customer is ready to pay the price for exceptional restaurant experiences.

Obviously, it is a smaller pool of consumers than the mass audience, but it exists – and not just in Delhi and Mumbai but also (and perhaps more so) in smaller towns that may have a lot of wealth, a lot of aspiration, but not enough avenues to spend. A top, niche restaurant that can cater to this segment of people, who want the best – at par with 'global' experiences – can work financially. And many do.

Since the pool of diners in India that is able to afford more expensive meals is much lower than in more mature restaurant markets, and because tourism is low, any restaurant that does not offer value to a customer will lose out. So, even if a restaurant is expensive, it has to offer enough value by way of top-quality ingredients, unusual cooking or top-notch creativity from its chef, as well as excellent ambience and service, for a consumer to be able to derive value from the experience.

Sadly, both are in scarce supply at the moment. A restaurant where the food and beverages are only average qualitatively, but which thinks its plush interiors can drive in customers willing to spend higher than the norm in that category, will always be in for a shock. The limited number of big spenders will not see enough value in returning to the place.

To add to the problem, many restaurants that want to be perceived as high-end or luxury seem to believe that big spaces and prime locations are going to be able to pull in customers repeatedly from the very same limited pool of people with both enough money and enough exposure to luxury dining.

Again, these restaurants usually fall flat because after the first exposure to novelty, customers simply don't return.

The mismatch between what the restaurant is offering and who it is reaching out to is really what causes most restaurants to fail.

As entrepreneur Anirban Blah, who travels the world to eat at top restaurants, told me once, 'Indians are not short of money. I think it is a supply-side constraint. I don't see many chefs doing really brave or innovative food. For a premium luxury experience, there needs to be a commitment to quality and innovation that doesn't really exist in the Indian food scene.'

It may be time to change that and up the quality of our restaurants at all levels, across all segments. As consumers evolve, travel more and begin to spend more in restaurants, they will demand better quality for their rupee – and restaurants must gear up for that.

PARTING WORDS

Indian restaurants have come a very long way from the time they were the haunts primarily of travellers, the working class, poets and drunks, as well as adventurous, sneaking students, and in general were frowned upon by the 'respectable' middle class that ate at home.

Today, eating out is such a huge part of our youth culture that it is difficult to imagine life without being able to frequent a restaurant at least once or twice week. However, there is a huge gap in the market for quality restaurants that deliver what they promise and are true to their concept. The larger Indian audience may evolve and begin to pay more for eating out as the years go by, and we may eventually have restaurants that can price their menus higher instead of being forced to play the discounts and deals game. On the flip side, given that delivery apps like Swiggy and Zomato are now playing the discount game, this may take many, many years.

However, it is my belief that even in the casual-dining, mid-market segment, which is growing the fastest in India, there is a lot of scope to up the quality of the product. It requires clear thinking and clear assessment by the restaurateurs as to what their strengths are, and what kind of cuisine and concept they would like to bring forth in keeping with their core beliefs, values and personalities, making for a more authentic experience for the target customers in turn. It requires a great deal of financial wisdom and planning, but above all, clarity on what a restaurateur's ambition is – to risk scale or to do smaller, higher-quality concepts that have the potential to develop into solid brands.

Above all, as the tricky Indian marketplace continues with all its contradictions and challenges by way of the frequently changing regulatory environment, rents and so on, there is a huge need for any first-time restaurateur to come in with a clear head. Shed those visions of glamour, sit down, learn from the examples of those who have trod this space before you, realize that it is a fickle and tricky business, and also the fact that you would need to be committed to it in a way quite similar to marriage or parenthood.

However, with the audience evolving and visiting restaurants becoming such a marker of pop culture, there is room today for all kinds of restaurants. A savvy restaurateur will be able to find an audience for whatever they want to do. If they are fiscally prudent, clear and consistent in their execution, and are able to set the quality of food and restaurant experience apart even slightly from the mediocrity that seems to exist today, they will be able to stand out and create a beloved brand. It's easier said than done, but not an impossible recipe to cook.

NOTES

1. In the Beginning

1. A fascinating account often quoted by historians of the Mughal period is by Thomas Roe, who had come to Jahangir's court representing Elizabeth I. In his correspondence available in books such as *The Embassy of Sir Thomas Roe to the Court of the Great Mogul 1615–1619* (edited by William Foster), Roe bitterly complains, 'They eate [sic] not willingly with us.' Roe apparently was invited just once to the home of a noble – Asaf Khan, Shah Jahan's brother-in-law. The table was full, but the host would not eat with his guest.
2. Malcom Murphy's *The Last Children of the Raj* and John Mitchell's *The Wheels of IND*, published in the early 20th century, paint a distinctive picture of rail travel and food during the Raj. Catering services are fully described in *The Illustrated Guide to the South Indian Railway* of 1900, which

gives details of arrangements for refreshment rooms at certain stations and the method of pre-ordering and reserving seating.

3. Vikram Doctor, 'Refreshing the Railways: Regional Food May Reinvent Pantry Cars', *Economic Times*, 5 December 2015. https://economictimes.indiatimes.com/blogs/onmyplate/refreshing-the-railways-regional-foods-may-reinvent-pantry-cars/
4. Raghu Dayal, 'Even Water in India Had a Religion', *The Hindu BusinessLine*, 22 March 2019. https://www.thehindubusinessline.com/opinion/even-water-in-india-had-a-religion/article26611705.ece#!
5. Anoothi Vishal, 'Partition Changed India's Food Cultures Forever', *Wire*, 14 August 2017. https://thewire.in/food/partition-food-punjab-mughlai-bengal
6. Harprasad Ray, 'The Chinese', *Banglapedia*. http://en.banglapedia.org/index.php?title=Chinese,_The

2. Of Failures and Successes

1. BBC News, 'Prescott and Conran Hospitality Group Goes Bust', 20 June 2018. https://www.bbc.com/news/business-44549715
2. BBC News, 'Carluccio's Rescue Plan Could Close 30 Restaurants', 31 May 2018. https://www.bbc.com/news/business-44315826
3. Danielle Isaac, 'Why High-End, Michelin Star Restaurants

Are Shutting Down in Singapore', *Singapore Business Review*, 18 June 2018. https://sbr.com.sg/food-beverage/exclusive/why-high-end-michelin-star-restaurants-are-shutting-down-in-singapore

4. Vincent Wood, 'Restaurant Insolvency Reaches Record High as More than 1,100 Businesses Go Bust', *Caterer*, 5 November 2018. https://www.thecaterer.com/articles/540813/restaurant-insolvency-reaches-record-high-as-more-than-1100-businesses-go-bust
5. David Brown, 'Fickle Diners Blamed as Record Number of Restaurants Go Bust', *Sunday Times*, 5 November 2018. https://www.thetimes.co.uk/article/fickle-diners-blamed-as-record-number-of-restaurants-go-bust-q009t6790
6. Ed Cumming, 'Restaurants Fail for Many Reasons – Don't Try to Pin This on Millennials', *Guardian*, 6 November 2018. https://www.theguardian.com/commentisfree/2018/nov/06/restaurants-fail-millennials-jamies-byron-gbk
7. Reeba Zachariah, 'Delhiites Dine Out the Most, but Bengaluru Splurges More', *Times of India*, 13 June 2019. https://timesofindia.indiatimes.com/india/delhiites-dine-out-the-most-but-bengaluru-splurges-more/articleshow/69764111.cms
8. Kristy Cooke, 'The UK Spent over £49bn on Eating and Drinking Out Last Year, *Kantar UK Insights*, 27 April 2018. https://uk.kantar.com/consumer/shoppers/2018/the-uk-spent-over-%C2%A349bn-on-eating-and-drinking-out-last-year/

9. Anumeha Chaturvedi and Varuni Khosla, 'Here Are Some Reasons Why Restaurants Run Out of Steam So Soon', *Economic Times*, 25 February 2017. https://economictimes.indiatimes.com/magazines/panache/lifestyle/here-are-the-reasons-why-restaurants-run-out-of-steam-so-soon/articleshow/57337106.cms?from=mdr

3. A Plateful of Personality

1. Nayantara Rai, 'Grand Old Restaurants in Delhi Get Better with Time', *India Today*, 14 November 2005. https://www.indiatoday.in/magazine/supplement/story/20051114-grand-old-restaurants-in-delhi-get-better-with-time-786633-2005-11-14
2. Diya Kohli, 'A.D. Singh: Sangria, Sushi and All That Jazz', *Mint*, 18 July 2017. https://www.livemint.com/Leisure/pdz2GdyJqwHMj5S5FLfEbP/AD-Singh-Sangria-sushi-and-all-that-jazz.html
3. PTI/*Mint*, 'Rabobank PE Fund Buys 40% Stake in Olive Bar and Kitchen for Rs 100 Crore', 28 December 2017. https://www.livemint.com/Companies/zOLQcsHamPng9VeeR9vuwN/Rabobank-PE-Fund-buys-40-stake-in-Olive-Bar-and-Kitchen-for.html
4. Tim Lewis, 'Claus Meyer: The Other Man from Noma', *Guardian*, 20 March 2016. https://www.theguardian.com/lifeandstyle/2016/mar/20/claus-meyer-the-other-man-from-noma-copenhagen-nordic-kitchen-recipes

5. Jay Cheshes, 'Claus Meyer's Food Empire', *Wall Street Journal*, 5 December 2013. https://www.wsj.com/articles/tk-1385412132
6. Debjyoti Roy, 'Sagar Ratna Founder Buys Out PE Firm India Equity Partners', *VCCircle*, 23 May 2017. https://www.vccircle.com/sagar-ratna-founder-buys-out-pe-firm-india-equity-partners/
7. Danielle Isaac, 'Why High-end Michelin-star Restaurants Are Shutting down in Singapore', *Singapore Business Review*, 18 June 2018. https://sbr.com.sg/food-beverage/exclusive/why-high-end-michelin-star-restaurants-are-shutting-down-in-singapore
8. Pete Wells, 'Why David Chang Matters', *New York Times*, 28 August 2018. https://www.nytimes.com/2018/08/28/dining/david-chang-kojin-toronto.html
9. Raaj Sanghvi, 'Why Bangkok's Most Popular Indian Restaurant, Gaggan, Has Shut Down', *Vogue India*, 26 August 2019. https://www.vogue.in/culture-and-living/content/gaggan-anand-bangkok-best-restaurants-in-asia
10. Soumya Gupta, 'Overcooked: Why the Stock of Anjan Chatterjee's Speciality Restaurants Went on the Slide', *ET Prime*, 11 December 2018. https://prime.economictimes.indiatimes.com/news/67025571/consumer/overcooked-why-the-stock-of-anjan-chatterjees-speciality-restaurants-went-on-the-slide
11. Katherine Doherty, 'P.F. Chang's Is Sold to TriArtisan Capital and Paulson', *Bloomberg*, 11 January 2019.

https://www.bloomberg.com/news/articles/2019-01-10/p-f-chang-s-said-to-be-sold-to-triartisan-capital-and-paulson

4. By the Numbers

1. Plimsoll, 'Restaurants (UK) – Industry Report', June 2019.
2. MCA, 'Dishoom Sees Profits Leap in 2018', 13 August 2019. https://www.mca-insight.com/results/dishoom-sees-profits-leap-in-2018/596563.article
3. *Guardian*, 'Wagamama Noodle Chain Sold to Frankie and Benny's Owner', 30 October 2018. https://www.theguardian.com/business/2018/oct/30/wagamama-noodle-chain-sold-frankie-and-bennys-owner-restaurant-group
4. España Global, 'Spanish Tourism Reaches a New Record in 2018', 18 January 2019. https://espanaglobal.gob.es/en/current-news/tourism/spanish-tourism-reaches-new-record-2018
5. Ministry of Tourism, Government of India, 'Indian Tourism Statistics at a Glance 2018'. http://tourism.gov.in/sites/default/files/Other/ITS_Glance_2018_Eng_Version_for_Mail.pdf

5. Slipping on Scale

1. The NRAI's 2019 report on the state of the industry has a different estimate, putting the average frequency at 6.6

times a month per person, but this includes even tea or coffee and not only meals.

2. Soumya Gupta, 'Overcooked: Why the Stock of Anjan Chatterjee's Speciality Restaurants Went on the Slide', *ET Prime*, 11 December 2018. https://prime.economictimes.indiatimes.com/news/67025571/consumer/overcooked-why-the-stock-of-anjan-chatterjees-speciality-restaurants-went-on-the-slide
3. Ben Martin, 'Pret a Manger Sold for £1.5 Billion to Germany's Deal-Hungry Reimann family', *Reuters*, 29 May 2018. https://uk.reuters.com/article/uk-pret-m-a-jab-holdings/pret-a-manger-sold-for-1-5-billion-to-germanys-deal-hungry-reimann-family-idUKKCN1IU017
4. Javier Espinoza and Eric Platt, 'Private Equity Races to Spend Record $2.5tn Cash Pile', *Financial Times*, 27 June 2019. https://www.ft.com/content/2f777656-9854-11e9-9573-ee5cbb98ed36
5. Loren Feldman, 'Danny Meyer Talks about His Fear of Growth and Why He Didn't Want to Run Shake Shack', *Forbes*, 7 January 2018. https://www.forbes.com/sites/lorenfeldman/2018/01/07/danny-meyer-talks-about-his-fear-of-growth-and-why-he-didnt-want-to-run-shake-shack/#7f65ad516d5e

6. Spicing It Up: Publicity, PR and Social Media

1. Rachel Hosie, 'How Instagram has Transformed the Restaurant Industry for Millennials', *Independent*, 11 April 2017. https://www.independent.co.uk/life-style/food-and-drink/millenials-restaurant-how-choose-instagram-social-media-where-eat-a7677786.html
2. Anoothi Vishal, 'Who Is the Winner at Food Awards?', *The Hindu*, 26 October 2018. https://www.thehindu.com/life-and-style/food/who-is-the-winner-at-food-awards/article25335449.ece
3. Sierra Tishgart, 'How Noma Became the Most Influential Restaurant in The World', *Grub Street*, 15 September 2015. http://www.grubstreet.com/2015/09/history-of-noma.html

8. What Do Customers Want?

1. IANS/*Mint*, '₹442 for Two Bananas Very Much Justified: Hoteliers' Association Explains Why', 30 July 2019. https://www.livemint.com/news/india/rs-442-for-two-bananas-very-much-justified-hoteliers-association-explains-why-1564492638024.html